Faith Languages
Thoughts for Each Day

Patrick M. Devitt

VERITAS

First published 2008 by
Veritas Publications
7/8 Lower Abbey Street
Dublin 1
Ireland
Email publications@veritas.ie
Website www.veritas.ie

ISBN 978 1 84730 121 5

First published on the Catholic portal site for Ireland,
www.catholicireland.net, and made available to parish and other websites
built by them on a daily basis from 2001 – 2005.

Extracts from the *Catechism of the Catholic Church*
© 2006 Libreria Editrice Vaticana

Designed by Vivienne Adu-Boahen
Printed in the Republic of Ireland by Betaprint, Dublin

Veritas books are printed on paper made from the wood pulp of managed forests.
For every tree felled, at least one tree is planted, thereby renewing natural resources.

Contents

Part Three: Life in Christ

Part 3, Section 1, Chapter 1 (3.1.1)

Part Four: Christian Prayer

Part 4, Section 1, Chapter 1 (4.1.1)

Preface

During the years 2001–2005, I posted a daily catechetical reflection on CatholicIreland.net. This was called CRED (Catechetical Reflections for Each Day). The idea for this project came to me quite suddenly, when I heard about the finding of a dead body in a suitcase in the Grand Canal, less than a mile from where I live. As I was cycling along Russell Street, I saw a few women standing on the canal bridge and pointing west. It was they who explained to me about the strange events of that day.

I couldn't help thinking about the person who had been so cruelly destroyed. Being a person of faith, I automatically connected these reflections to my prayers and wondered where God was in all of this. Christian faith believes in a God who speaks to the human race through the events of every day. What might God be saying to us today through this and other occurrences? My *Catechism of the Catholic Church (CCC)* was nearby as I wrote these reflections, and I also began to wonder how earlier Catholic Christians had faced such issues as sudden death, illness, warfare etc. Catechesis involves listening for echoes of God in the past and in the present.

I decided to keep up this series of reflections (calling them 'CRED') in a spirit of faith ('*credo*' means I believe). I began to search through the *CCC* in order to find traditional phrases to illuminate my thoughts about the events of each day as they touched my heart, mind and imagination. I added these selected quotes from the *CCC* to the end of my own personal, daily reflections. God speaks through the bits and pieces of every day. CRED is one person's attempt to record something of God's soothing and challenging voice. Readers of CRED may be encouraged to do likewise, listening to God in their own lives.

After CRED was no longer posted daily, the entire resource was kept available in archive form. I was able to use this resource while teaching undergraduate and postgraduate religion teachers in the Mater Dei Institute of Education. It was very useful for one of my third year courses: 'The Catechism: Resource for Junior Cert and Leaving Cert Religious Education'. Many students found it very helpful when preparing lessons during teaching practice; it gave them a range of short stories that made concrete the often abstract topics they were being asked to teach. Postgraduates have also been able to draw upon CRED in their ongoing research.

A thought began to germinate in my mind: what about selecting some of this material for publication? At first, I considered using the existing CRED system of categorisation. Every daily CRED item has been categorised under the following headings: Morals, Sacraments, Christian Vocation, Prayer, Sunday Gospels, Saints, God the Father, Jesus Christ Son of God, God the Holy Spirit, Books, The Human Condition and Church. Might not one of these provide the basis for a book?

Then I had an idea. Why not change the perspective entirely? Instead of thinking like CRED (which moves *from* today's events down to a paragraph from the *CCC*), I decided to start each item of my book with a text of the CCC and place this text above its connected CRED reflection. I spent some time reading my much marked CCC, and selected about one in every ten paragraphs from beginning to end. This allowed the structural logic of that magisterial document to shape my book. The headings and major sub-headings of the CCC have also been integrated into the text, again to help the reader's progress.

The present book consists of reflections on about 250 of the 2,865 paragraphs in the CCC. Once my reflection began to move from CCC texts *down* to daily incidents, I then saw the value of going even further: each reflection then moved into a scriptural text. These were easy to identify, as they were often noted in the CCC.

What has emerged is a meditation on the Catholic Faith, which uses three distinct languages: the theological language of the CCC, the catechetical language of daily life and the Word of God in Scripture. These three faith languages provide a form of meditation for everyday life.

Prologue

> This catechism aims at presenting an organic synthesis
> of the essential and fundamental contents of Catholic
> doctrine, as regards both faith and morals, in the light
> of the Second Vatican Council and the whole of the
> Church's Tradition. (CCC 11)

The Easter garden is in the usual place, down left in the
sanctuary of the church of St Agatha, North William Street.
The focal point is the bare cross, with a white cloth draped
around it, and discreetly lit up from behind. A fountain of
water plays among green shrubs, and a few rabbits peep up
in amazement. Hidden from view, a small goldfish swims in
the pond. He belongs to Paddy Tucker's daughter and is
called *ichthus* (the Greek word for fish).

Some people find the garden intrusive and unwelcome, but
surely the beauty of God's creation is a very apt sign of the
beauty of the resurrection. And *ichthus* reminds us how the
early Christians painted fish on the walls of the catacombs
where they buried their dead in the hope of eternal life. The
letters are the initials of the Greek phrase: 'Jesus Christ,
God's son, saviour'. This is the heart of Easter faith, hope and
love. This is God's new creation.

> After Jesus had spoken these words, he looked up
> to heaven and said, 'Father, the hour has come; glorify
> your Son so that the Son may glorify you, since
> you have given him authority over all people,
> to give eternal life to all whom you have given him.
> And this is eternal life, that they may know you, the
> only true God, and Jesus Christ whom you have sent'.
> (John 17:1-3)

By design, this Catechism does not set out to provide the adaptation ... required by the differences of culture, age, spiritual maturity, and social and ecclesial condition among all those to whom it is addressed. Such indispensable adaptations are the responsibility of particular catechisms and, even more, of those who instruct the faithful. (CCC 24)

The sower went out to sow his seed and, as he sowed, some seed fell by the side of the road, other seed fell on rocks, other seed fell among thorns, but other seed fell on good soil. The seed, according to Jesus, is the Word of God. Falling on different people, it bears fruit very differently. The Word is a power for life, but for some people no life flows from their listening to God's Word.

Jim Gallagher has written a fine book on catechesis, entitled *Soil for the Seed*. Instead of giving a theological account of the seed (Word) and explaining what that Word means, his book refers more to the recipients of the Word (the variety of different soils refer to the great diversity of God's people on earth). Being different from one another justifies their receiving a different version of the Word. Is there then a danger of perversion of the Word?

For as the rain and the snow come down from heaven, and do not return there until they have watered the earth, making it bring forth and sprout, giving seed to the sower and bread to the eater, so shall my word be that goes out from my mouth; it shall not return to me empty, but it shall accomplish that which I purpose, and succeed in the thing for which I sent it. (Isaiah 55:10-11)

PART ONE

The Profession of Faith

Man's Capacity for God

> The desire for God is written in the human heart,
> because man is created by God and for God; and
> God never ceases to draw man to himself.
> (CCC 27)

It's not often one reads a book on religious faith written by someone who has taught both English Literature and Fundamental Theology. Such a work came my way recently: Michael Paul Gallagher's *Dive Deeper: The Human Poetry of Faith*. His thesis is simple: one major faith crisis today derives from the fact that religion and life have separated from each other. Where once the hungers of life found nourishment in the images and symbols of religion, now religious language resonates little with inner feelings.

In order to reconnect life and religion, Gallagher suggests that we 'dive deep' into the central human experiences of friendship, failure, tragedy, silence and normality. Through the words of selected poets and novelists, he helps us explore this inner human terrain and discover its hopes and fears. This 'deep diving' allows us to listen attentively to the God-story of one who enters fully into life and death, in order to show us the loving passion of the God who creates and restores us.

> As a deer longs for flowing streams, so my soul
> longs for you, O God. (Psalm 42:1)

> In defending the ability of human reason to know God, the Church is expressing her confidence in the possibility of speaking about him to all men and with all men, and therefore of dialogue with other religions, with philosophy and science, as well as with unbelievers and atheists. (CCC 39)

It was a usual Monday night on RTÉ, and on came *Questions and Answers*. When John Bowman asked Robert Ballagh to comment on the Pope, Ballagh graciously declined, pleading his lack of belief. He did, however, make a brief reference to the barefooted preacher from Nazareth, in whose footsteps each Pope must follow. Here was true art: Ballagh's few simple words were more eloquent than a long speech.

One of the greatest changes in recent Catholic thinking is the movement from condemnation of unbelief to a recognition of the presence of the Holy Spirit, even in the heart of non-believers. According to the Second Vatican Council, God is mysteriously at work in every human being and, since God is beauty, truth and goodness, wherever people create beauty, search for truth and live good lives, God is with them, enriching them and drawing them towards full human flourishment.

> Then Paul stood in front of the Areopagus and said, 'Athenians, I see how extremely religious you are in every way. For as I went through the city and looked carefully at the objects of your worship, I found among them an altar with the inscription, "To an unknown god". What therefore you worship as unknown, this I proclaim to you'. (Acts 17:22-23)

> We can name God only by taking creatures as our starting point, and in accordance with our limited human ways of knowing and thinking. (CCC 40)

A Manhattan teenager, who had committed crime and was in custody awaiting trial, put pen to paper and rewrote Psalm 22. He had never known a shepherd, or ever seen a sheep. He had heard of people living in the desert, but he could only imagine the thrill of green pastures and the pleasure of running streams. He wrote about what he knew. 'The Lord', he said, 'is my probation officer. He digs me and looks out for me and stands up for me.'

Downtown Manhattan became a symbol. The rubble that covered the missing five thousand innocent people became an indictment of terror and violence. But the response of the city was superb. The members of the fire department continued to search, hoping to find someone still alive. With great courage and in spite of constant threat to their own lives, they sought out the dead bodies. Like the woman searching for the lost drachma, or the father running out to seek his two sons, they are a reminder of God's compassionate heart. If sin can be seen as a kind of spiritual death, then God must be a firefighter, seeking the lost and searching for the dead.

> For from the greatness and beauty of created things comes a corresponding perception of their Creator. (Wisdom 13:5)

God Comes to Meet Man

> It pleased God, in his goodness and wisdom, to reveal himself and to make known the mystery of his will. His will was that men should have access to the Father, through Christ, the Word made flesh, in the Holy Spirit, and thus become sharers in the divine nature (Dei Verbum, 2). (CCC 51)

Jews have always believed in a God who spoke a word to them; their God was a God who refused to stay silent, a God who continued to communicate with them, no matter where they were and no matter how far they wandered from the paths of righteousness. God spoke his word in a vibrant manner through creation, but in an even more dynamic way through the history of the Jewish people. In each case God was saying, 'I want to create life and I want all people to live life to the full'.

When John the Evangelist said that the Word of God became flesh in Jesus of Nazareth, he was making an extraordinary claim. He was saying that the beauty of creation, as well as the liberating power of God calling his people out of the slavery of Egypt into the milk and honey of his Promised Land, are now focussed in the human life of a Jewish carpenter. The grandeur and majesty of God are now fully on display in this human heart. To hear God we simply listen to Jesus.

> In the beginning was the Word, and the Word was with God, and the Word was God. And the Word became flesh and lived among us, and we have seen his glory, the glory as of a father's only son, full of grace and truth. (John 1:1, 14)

> The prophets proclaim a radical redemption of the People of God, purification from all their infidelities, a salvation which will include all the nations. Above all, the poor and humble of the Lord will bear this hope. *(CCC 64)*

The Church needs all sorts of people. Because there is so much wrong with the world, we need a constant supply of prophets to tell us this harsh truth and to challenge us to put injustices right. But we also need the voice of the one who compliments us for things well done and regularly inspires us to keep doing right. St Barnabas is famous for being a person who encouraged others.

At this moment, the Catholic Church in many parts of the world is under attack because of the manner in which many of its bishops mishandled child sex abuse allegations against certain clergy. After this storm has passed, the need for some new Barnabas will be very obvious. The Church, Christ's little flock, will need to hear a voice of encouragement, calling her forward into the unknown future.

> When the poor and needy seek water, and there is none, and their tongue is parched with thirst, I the LORD will answer them, I the God of Israel will not forsake them. (Isaiah 41:17)

> Tradition is to be distinguished from the various theological, disciplinary, or devotional traditions, born in the local churches over time. These are the particular forms, adapted to different places and times, in which the great Tradition is expressed. (CCC 83)

Eamon Duffy, an Irishman born in Dundalk, is a famous Church historian, now teaching in Cambridge. He recently published a short book called *Faith of our Fathers: Reflections on Catholic Tradition*. This consisted largely of short articles he had published earlier in the English journal, *Priests and People*. We read it in our theology book circle and most of us found it very helpful. Duffy claims he is not a theologian, but he writes beautifully about theological issues. This book merits careful reading.

In particular, I loved his analysis of Catholic tradition as a resource for creative engagement with new challenges to the faith. I am also convinced of his argument for making fasting and abstinence a communal ritual rather than a private devotion. But where I empathised most with him was in his plea for more anger and grief to be allowed in our funeral services. In celebrating the resurrection of the body, we must also lament the destruction of death.

> For I handed on to you as of first importance what I in turn had received: that Christ died for our sins in accordance with the scriptures, and that he was buried, and that he was raised on the third day in accordance with the scriptures, and that he appeared to Cephas, then to the twelve. (1 Corinthians 15:3-5)

> All the faithful share in understanding and handing on revealed truth. They have received the anointing of the Holy Spirit, who instructs them and guides them into all truth. (CCC 91)

Thomas Aquinas was one of the most outstanding saint-theologians the Church has known. He emphasised the unity of truth, convinced that human reason and Christian faith, though approaching wisdom from different perspectives, can never ultimately be in disagreement. Intellectual life and spiritual life are but two sides of the one human coin. A true intellectual recognises that the mystery of God (or absolute truth) can never be exhausted by any human exploration.

In his constant searching for deeper insights, Aquinas did not neglect any source of knowledge. He drew from the rediscovered texts of Aristotle a realist philosophy to counterbalance the traditional idealism of Plato. He assessed all positions he disagreed with, not to condemn them, but rather to learn whatever truth could be gleaned from them. His example might be helpful today in conflict resolution.

> When the Spirit of truth comes, he will guide you into all the truth; for he will not speak on his own, but will speak whatever he hears, and he will declare to you the things that are to come. He will glorify me, because he will take what is mine and declare it to you. All that the Father has is mine. For this reason I said that he will take what is mine and declare it to you. (John 16:13-15)

In Sacred Scripture, God speaks to man in a human way. To interpret Scripture correctly, the reader must be attentive to what the human authors truly wanted to affirm, and to what God wanted to reveal to us by their words. (CCC 109)

He was told he could 'eat, drink and be merry', but then he began to worry about the 'forbidden fruit' that he had eaten 'at the eleventh hour'. Though he was truly 'the salt of the earth', he allowed others 'to cast the first stone', which they did with glee. As they led him out 'like a lamb to the slaughter', he asked ironically, 'Am I my brother's keeper?' Then the issue of 'blood money' began to frighten him, so he figured that 'the writing was on the wall'.

The Bible has given the English language some of its most powerful phrases. People often speak 'bible-talk' without noticing what they are doing. This is one good educational reason for requiring pupils to attend to the Biblical record. Of course, a more important justification for reading the Bible is a reason of the heart: to people of faith, the Bible is God's life-giving word in beautiful human language, which invites a profound change of heart.

All scripture is inspired by God and is useful for teaching, for reproof, for correction, and for training in righteousness, so that everyone who belongs to God may be proficient, equipped for every good work. (2 Timothy 3:16-17)

> The Old Testament is an indispensable part of Sacred Scripture. Its books are divinely inspired and retain a permanent value, for the Old Covenant has never been revoked. (CCC 121)

St Edith Stein is one of the most recently canonised saints. She was born a Jew, but lapsed into unbelief and agnosticism. Under the influence of some ordinary Catholics she met in her work, she converted to the Catholic faith. Later on she wrote many impressive spiritual works and lived as a contemplative sister, until she was arrested by the Nazis and condemned to the gas chambers for being a Jew.

At the time of her canonisation she was called a martyr. This generated much opposition in some Jewish quarters. Because she was killed for being a Jew, many Jews felt that her deepest identity (as a Jew) was lost sight of in her being raised to the altars of the Church. The close relation between Jews and Christians, which is a factor in modern Catholic teaching, does not and probably cannot easily remove the memory of so much anti-Semitism in the past. St Edith has been declared a patroness of Europe. What purpose can this declaration serve, as modern Europeans try to transcend the hatred and bigotry of the past?

> 'For a brief moment I abandoned you, but with great compassion I will gather you. In overflowing wrath for a moment I hid my face from you, but with everlasting love I will have compassion on you,' says the LORD, your Redeemer ... 'For the mountains may depart and the hills be removed, but my steadfast love shall not depart from you, and my covenant of peace shall not be removed,' says the LORD, who has compassion on you. (Isaiah 54:7-8, 10)

> The ministry of the Word, too – pastoral preaching, catechetics and all forms of Christian instruction, among which the liturgical homily should take pride of place – is healthily nourished and thrives in holiness through the Word of Scripture (Dei Verbum, 24). (CCC 132)

Padraig O'Sullivan was a seminarian for the Dublin Diocese and a student at Maynooth. When he was on pastoral placement in our parish. Fr Liam Rigney invited him to speak to the parish, at all the weekend Masses. When he had spoken at the eleven o'clock Mass, at which I presided, the people clapped for him. I was not surprised: he spoke with great simplicity and conviction about his decision to study for the priesthood and the variety of responses he got from his family and friends.

I thought back to a comment made years ago by Desmond Fennell, who was describing his experience of listening to sermons. He summed up his general dissatisfaction as follows: 'What I miss most in sermons is a man talking'. Fennell was not searching for eloquence or rhetorical flourishes in church, all he wanted was to know that the priest really meant what he was saying, and said it in a convincing manner. Padraig has made a very good start.

> He must have a firm grasp of the word that is trustworthy in accordance with the teaching, so that he may be able both to preach with sound doctrine and to refute those who contradict it. (Titus 1:9)

> By his Revelation, 'the invisible God, from the fullness of his love, addresses men as his friends, and moves among them, in order to invite and receive them into his own company' (Dei Verbum, 2). (CCC 142)

The Gospel tells of a king who invites people to a wedding feast for his son. In one sense, God is like us. When we invite someone to a wedding, we immediately think of those who have a special place in our hearts. All those invited to this strange wedding feast by God must be very special to God. We are surely part of this people, and for this we give thanks, over and over again, in every Mass.

In another sense, God's ways are definitely not our ways. We put limits on those we will ask; God, on the other hand, asks both good and bad. We calculate our level of generosity; God is generous without limit. We are good towards some and nasty towards others; God loves everybody with the same infinite compassion. But even God expects something in return. To respond well to God's invitation, as we approach his wedding feast we should don the clothes of respect and gratitude.

> The kingdom of heaven may be compared to a king who gave a wedding banquet for his son. He sent his slaves to call those who had been invited to the wedding banquet, but they would not come. Again he sent other slaves, saying, 'Tell those who have been invited: Look, I have prepared my dinner, my oxen and my fat calves have been slaughtered, and everything is ready; come to the wedding banquet'. (Matthew 22:2-4)

> Believing is possible only by grace and the interior helps of the Holy Spirit. But it is no less true that believing is an authentically human act. (CCC 154)

Faith in God is a strange commodity. For millennia, the great religions have all claimed a monopoly on it. Jews were so convinced that they were God's chosen people that they could not believe God was calling other people to faith in him. Jesus clearly had problems with the idea that a Canaanite lady could show such faith in God. Christian theology spoke about 'no salvation outside the Church'. Christian liturgy once referred to Jews as 'infidels' (people outside the realm of faith). Muslims call people of other religions by the title 'infidel' (unfaithful person).

Faith in God seems to be found everywhere on earth. Its shape and form, its language and culture may vary from nation to nation, but in its heart it remains the same. Faith in God comes from the promptings of God, to which all believers respond, some more generously than others, but all with some integrity.

> And Jesus answered him, 'Blessed are you, Simon son of Jonah! For flesh and blood has not revealed this to you, but my Father in heaven'. (Matthew 16:17)

> Methodical research in all branches of knowledge ... can never conflict with the faith, because the things of the world and the things of faith derive from the same God (Gaudium et spes, 36). (CCC 159)

Since the beginning of recorded time people have contracted malaria from mosquito bites and millions have died of the disease. Though some countries have eliminated the scourge, the disease still kills many children and poor folk in the developing world. A wonderful scientific event has just taken place: the two genomes of the anopheles mosquito (the carrier) and the parasite that causes malaria have been published in the research journals, *Nature* and *Science*. The world now has the information to develop drugs to prevent malaria and, therefore, save countless lives.

This is a time for celebration. People are cooperating in the search for cures to fatal diseases, human science and technology is being used in the furtherance of human well-being; this is creativity that mirrors the life-enhancing work of God – no matter how we describe what is going on, it is good to be here to witness it and shout about it from the rooftops, especially as we know that war continues throughout the world.

> It is he who made the earth by his power, who established the world by his wisdom, and by his understanding stretched out the heavens. (Jeremiah 10:12)

> Each believer is thus a link in the great chain of believers. I cannot believe without being carried by the faith of others, and by my faith I help support others in the faith. (CCC 166)

Traditionally, he is called 'doubting Thomas', and this is a fairly accurate account of his behaviour during the first Easter week. But Thomas, who first absents himself from the gathering of the faithful, finally joins them in worship a week later on this Low Sunday. And how he is changed! The unbeliever who had resolutely refused to believe the word of his brothers and sisters now becomes a firm believer.

His act of faith, 'My Lord and my God', is a profoundly personal statement of his commitment to Jesus Christ, the risen Lord. But this faith is possible only within the community of worshipping believers. His personal credo is also very definitely the credo of the gathered community. Christian faith can be lived only by free persons, and can be lived fully only within a believing and supporting community.

> A week later his disciples were again in the house, and Thomas was with them. Although the doors were shut, Jesus came and stood among them and said, 'Peace be with you.' Then he said to Thomas, 'Put your finger here and see my hands. Reach out your hand and put it in my side. Do not doubt but believe.' Thomas answered him, 'My Lord and my God!' (John 20:26-28)

> God loves his people more than a bridegroom
> his beloved. (CCC 219)

Swallows were flying in and out of the café beside the pool. Some guests left bits of cheese and crumbs of bread for the birds to eat. The swallows were being well cared for. Here was an echo of the consoling words of Jesus, 'You are more important than many swallows'. This phrase is a beautiful act of faith in God's care for all people.

The God of creation is generous to the point of distraction. Every creature finds in the world more than enough for survival and flourishment. Human beings are no different. Somehow, God's providence ensures that we have more than we need to survive. Though we do meet hurdles that we must cross, the hand of God's grace is there to catch us as we fall and restore us to life once again.

> And I will take you for my wife forever; I will
> take you for my wife in righteousness and in
> justice, in steadfast love, and in mercy. I will take
> you for my wife in faithfulness; and you shall
> know the LORD. (Hosea 2:19-20)

The Implications of Faith in One God: 'It means living in thanksgiving'. (CCC 224)

My father was in the Coronary Care Unit in Tallaght Hospital for nearly a week before he died. He never stopped talking about the nurses who were looking after him: 'If they were my own daughters, they couldn't have done more for me'. One day, while I was visiting, a nurse approached and he asked her name. She said, 'Gail' and immediately he responded, 'That's very strange, you're so calm'. He always loved playing with the meaning of words.

Gratitude was Dad's middle name. Nobody who ever did even the smallest favour for him was ever forgotten, and he remembered to thank God daily for all his blessings. When he went to Mass on Sundays, it was no more than a summary of the week that had passed. He prayed devoutly for forgiveness, listened intently to the reading of the Word of God, gave thanks to the Father for raising His Son, Jesus Christ, and then reverently ate the bread of life.

> For who sees anything different in you? What do you have that you did not receive? And if you received it, why do you boast as if it were not a gift? (1 Corinthians 4:7)

> The Trinity is a mystery of faith in the strict sense, one of the 'mysteries that are hidden in God, which can never be known unless they are revealed by God' (Dei Filius, 4). (CCC 237)

God our Father, you are the radiant sun of our lives. Though clouds of sinfulness often hide you from our eyes, you can still light up our lives and warm our hearts. Your Son, Jesus Christ, is the light of the world. Your Holy Spirit is the fire that warms our hearts and melts our resistance, and joins us together as one faithful people. We are eternally grateful, O Divine Father, that you have sent your Son to redeem and save us. We are grateful too that you have given to us your own Holy Spirit, to make us like you: holy and united, a faithful people.

We are proud today to state, in halting words, the central truth of our faith: you God are one God. One God, you are Father, Son and Holy Spirit. Before your mystery, before your light and warmth we are silent and without words.

> Now the eleven disciples went to·Galilee, to the mountain to which Jesus had directed them. When they saw him, they worshiped him; but some doubted. And Jesus came and said to them, 'All authority in heaven and on earth has been given to me. Go therefore and make disciples of all nations, baptising them in the name of the Father and of the Son and of the Holy Spirit, and teaching them to obey everything that I have commanded you. And remember, I am with you always, to the end of the age.' (Matthew 28:16-20)

The divine persons are really distinct from one another. 'God is one but not solitary.' (CCC 254)

On the feast of the Holy Trinity, we celebrated Mass in St Nicolò parish church near the centre of Verona. After the gospel we had an unusual few moments of reflection. A screen was erected before the altar, and behind it stood a local priest, well trained in mime. We saw only his two hands above the screen, as they danced around each other like Punch and Judy. We were enthralled.

The two hands were mirror images of one another, and yet they were strangely diverse. They never stopped moving and shaping up to each other. They were alive together in a startlingly seductive waltz. Then they appeared to embrace, but it was tender eros. Immediately they became one, entwined in the form of a fluttering dove. But soon they disconnected and the dance began all over again.

The grace of the Lord Jesus Christ, the love of God, and the communion of the Holy Spirit be with all of you. (2 Corinthians 13:13)

> The whole divine economy is the common work of the three divine persons. (CCC 258)

Two works of art in Verona, each dealing with the crucifixion of Christ – a huge one in St Zeno's and a small one in the Museum at Castelvecchio – caught my attention. In each of them the Father was represented at the very top; under this figure hovered the Spirit-dove; and lower down came the face of the suffering Jesus. The artists who painted these pictures believed that God the Father, God the Holy Spirit and God the Son were all involved somehow in the death of Jesus on the cross.

Although we profess our faith every Sunday in a triune God, sometimes we forget we are Trinitarians. We are happy to say that Jesus went freely to his death on Calvary, but less ready to profess that the Father loved us so much as to give his beloved Son up to death for our sakes. We rarely think of Calvary as the moment in which the Father and the Son jointly poured their Spirit upon us.

> Grace to you and peace from God our Father and the Lord Jesus Christ. Blessed be the God and Father of our Lord Jesus Christ, who has blessed us in Christ with every spiritual blessing in the heavenly places, just as he chose us in Christ before the foundation of the world to be holy and blameless before him in love. He destined us for adoption as his children through Jesus Christ, according to the good pleasure of his will, to the praise of his glorious grace that he freely bestowed on us in the Beloved. (Galatians 6:2-6)

> Faith in God the Father Almighty can be put to the test by the experience of evil and suffering. (CCC 272)

I lost a good night's sleep one Sunday because of a bomb scare. Somebody alerted the police to a suspicious box in the nearby phone booth. My dreams were shattered by the noise of the doorbell, but when I approached my front door (thinking that burglars were back again) I was very glad to meet the young Gárda officer, who explained that everybody in the street was being evacuated for safety reasons, while the bomb experts could do their work.

It was very efficient, no bomb was found, and we got back to bed tired but relieved. This was not so for the people in southern Italy, whose village was flattened by earth tremors and whose elementary school collapsed killing twenty-six young children. Their tragedy is a bitter cross, made all the heavier by the knowledge that the school was a modern building, and that most medieval buildings were able to withstand the power of the moving earth. Needless death, perhaps due to human negligence, is impossible to comprehend.

> For Jews demand signs and Greeks desire wisdom, but we proclaim Christ crucified, a stumbling block to Jews and foolishness to Gentiles, but to those who are the called, both Jews and Greeks, Christ the power of God and the wisdom of God. For God's foolishness is wiser than human wisdom, and God's weakness is stronger than human strength. (1 Corinthians 1:22-25)

> [Scientific] discoveries invite us to even greater admiration for the greatness of the Creator, prompting us to give him thanks for all his works and for the understanding and wisdom he gives to scholars and researchers. (CCC 283)

The young scientist competition came around once again, and I was thrilled to read that Ronan (a young friend, just fifteen) had won first prize in his section. Encouragement of scientific work is an imperative. Even those with scientific ability need to be regularly affirmed in their tedious labour. To receive a prize and positive criticism from examiners, and to have the honour of victory are all as important as food and drink. They are nourishment for the human spirit.

Because the relationship between religion and science is healthier now than in the past, people of faith and people of science can respect each other's varied perspectives. However, it is wrong to think they are two entirely separate endeavours. It is hard to imagine how any science would come into being unless one had faith in the intelligibility of the world. Equally, a faith without some feel for scientific research might miss the mysterious core of reality.

> May God grant me to speak with judgement, and to have thoughts worthy of what I have received; for he is the guide even of wisdom and the corrector of the wise. For both we and our words are in his hand, as are all understanding and skill in crafts. For it is he who gave me unerring knowledge of what exists, to know the structure of the world and the activity of the elements. (Wisdom 7:15-17)

> The existence of God the Creator can be known with certainty through his works, by the light of human reason, even if this knowledge is often obscured and disfigured by error. (CCC 286)

Below the north face of Mullaghcleevaun lies a tiny corrie lake. It was the mid point of our monthly walk. Resting for a short while, we noticed the huge granite boulders scattered all around, dropped by the melting, departing glacier ten thousand years ago. In this hidden place of wild beauty, with only a gurgling water sound to harmonise with the bird shrieks, it was easy to believe in God.

Other evidence of God surprised us on the way back. In spite of the marvellous camouflage of their dark brown coats, the small white rumps of a herd of darting deer gave their position away, reminding us of the way God darts in and out of our dreary lives, giving us a glimpse of white and beckoning us to pursue. A plane could be heard cutting through the still air: God's greatest creations can fly.

> By faith we understand that the worlds were prepared by the word of God, so that what is seen was made from things that are not visible. (Hebrews 11:3)

> The universe, created in and by the eternal Word, the 'image of the invisible God', is destined for and addressed to man, himself created in the 'image of God' and called to a personal relationship with God. (CCC 299)

The heritage centre in the middle of the Sperrin Mountains has a walk-through, audio-visual display to explain the surrounding countryside. One strolls through time, as it were, confronting the major changes that have occurred locally. Though many people have a vivid memory of the ghostly grocer who explains the customs of the past, my fondest memory is the images of huge mountains being worn down by the ice.

The low hills of today, so beautiful to view, were once gigantic peaks of Himalayan proportion. Then came the interminable Ice Age, with mile-thick ice covering the whole of the Northern Hemisphere, and eventually the thaw and then the movement of glaciers that gave the countryside its shape today. Long before people arrived to hunt and farm and put their own pattern on the landscape, God's millennia had been working steadily before them, creating a natural work of art.

> He is the image of the invisible God, the firstborn of all creation; for in him all things in heaven and on earth were created, things visible and invisible, whether thrones or dominions or rulers or powers – all things have been created through him and for him. (Colossians 1:15-16)

> With infinite power God could always create something better. But with infinite wisdom and goodness God freely willed to create a world 'in a state of journeying' towards its ultimate perfection. (CCC 310)

Life of Pi is Yann Martel's novel about a very long sea journey involving a young Indian boy and a Royal Bengal tiger in a small lifeboat. It claims to tell a story so good it will make you believe in God. Whether this claim is valid or not, I cannot tell. But millions of people may accept the claim, for the book has become a bestseller all over the world. What is so attractive about this strange story of survival?

Drawing on his wide knowledge of animal behaviour, learned in his father's zoo in Pondicherry, Pi tames the tiger by establishing his own presence in his space on the boat. Then he gives the tiger enough to eat and drink. This continues for most of a year at sea. Maybe people like this celebration of human superiority: the tiny boy tames the monster beast. Perhaps, though, the story is a parable about humans learning to coexist in small spaces cheek by jowl. If it is, maybe God is the hidden actor, sensed at work in conflict resolution.

> We know that all things work together for good for those who love God, who are called according to his purpose. (Romans 8:28)

> St Augustine says: 'Angel is the name of their office, not of their nature ...' With their whole beings the angels are servants and messengers of God. (CCC 329)

The feast of the Archangels Michael, Gabriel and Raphael is a challenge to human sophistication. In a world where we pride ourselves on discovering the mysteries of nature through scientific research, talk of angels invites us to recognise an even deeper mystery at the heart of all reality, the mystery we call God. To say that God sends his angels is to recognise that God has taken the initiative and makes his presence felt in our world. In other words, God is a revealing God, and God's angels reveal to us the very heart of God.

Names are powerful messages. Michael, Gabriel and Raphael all have 'el' in common, the old Hebrew word for God. Michael is a rhetorical shout, 'Who is like God?' The early Christians who named rocky fortresses after St Michael had this supportive, sustaining, rock-like power of God in mind. Gabriel means 'the strength of God' and suggests someone who interprets God's messianic messages for humans. Raphael means 'the healing of God' and, while reminding us of Tobias whose blindness was cured, it also suggests the full salvation that only God can give.

> The LORD has established his throne in the heavens, and his kingdom rules over all. Bless the LORD, O you his angels, you mighty ones who do his bidding, obedient to his spoken word. Bless the LORD, all his hosts, his ministers that do his will. (Psalms 103:19-21)

> Nothing exists that does not owe its existence to God the Creator. The world began when God's word drew it out of nothingness. (CCC 338)

Even in its darker form, before the restorers gave us back its brilliant colours, the fresco on the ceiling of the Sistine Chapel was truly remarkable. Ross King has recently published an account of this work of art, which tells how Pope Julius invited Michelangelo the sculptor to complete the painting in one of Rome's major chapels. *Michelangelo and the Pope's Ceiling* is as much about politics, religion and corruption as it is about art, creativity and beauty. Therein lies its strength as a modern novel.

Having read it recently, I was fascinated to learn how frescoes are made, and also to discover that the artist would have been standing with his head bent back while applying the paint to the vault (not at all a pleasant pose). What really surprised me, though, was the fact that Michelangelo's image of God the Creator confused one bishop when first he saw it: all he noticed was 'an old man, in the middle of the ceiling, who is represented in the act of flying through the air'.

> Then God said, 'Let us make humankind in our image, according to our likeness; and let them have dominion over the fish of the sea, and over the birds of the air, and over the cattle, and over all the wild animals of the earth, and over every creeping thing that creeps upon the earth.' So God created humankind in his image, in the image of God he created them; male and female he created them. (Genesis 1:26-27)

> The beauty of creation reflects the infinite beauty of the Creator and ought to inspire the respect and submission of man's intellect and will. (CCC 341)

Anthony had a look of quiet joy in his eyes when he told me the good news about Mary Rose, his wife, who was expecting their first baby in May. We were out beagling at Lacken, near Blessington. The first half hour was uneventful, then the hounds caught the scent of a deer and chased through the trees up the hill, over the fence, out into open country and down towards the farms in Lugnagun. As we raced down together, Anthony and I were both entranced by the nearby peaks.

Looking east we could see Sorrel, and further away the sun shone on the summit of Mullaghcleevaun. Anthony spoke excitedly about the way he so much enjoys coming up into the Wicklow Mountains from the plains of Kildare. It's good for the spirit to come into the uplands; it's uplifting, inspirational, enjoyable and refreshing. I could empathise with him, though I'm no farmer and come from Dublin.

> You set the earth on its foundations, so that it shall never be shaken. You cover it with the deep as with a garment; the waters stood above the mountains. At your rebuke they flee; at the sound of your thunder they take to flight. They rose up to the mountains, ran down to the valleys to the place that you appointed for them. (Psalms 104:5-8)

> Being in the image of God the human individual possesses the dignity of a person, who is not just something, but someone. (CCC 357)

What are the key values that underpin any educational service? That was one of the debating topics with our third year undergraduate students. We felt that academic excellence and elitism were central to the system in Japan, while developing self-confidence and lateral thinking seemed crucial in the USA. We were not sure how to rate Ireland. Perhaps we manifest a combination of the two.

No education process can be value free. Its values may be explicit or implicit, but they are always truly there, shaping the enterprise from top to bottom. Given the Christian understanding of human beings as made in the image of God, it follows that genuine Christian education is bound to be religious, in the sense of trying to foster the religious faith of the learners. How we understand people must be reflected in how we educate them.

> The God who made the world and everything in it, he who is Lord of heaven and earth, does not live in shrines made by human hands, nor is he served by human hands, as though he needed anything, since he himself gives to all mortals life and breath and all things. From one ancestor he made all nations to inhabit the whole earth, and he allotted the times of their existence and the boundaries of the places where they would live, so that they would search for God and perhaps grope for him and find him – though indeed he is not far from each one of us. (Acts 17:24-27)

> The human body shares in the dignity of 'the image of God': it is a human body precisely because it is animated by a spiritual soul, and it is the whole human person that is intended to become, in the body of Christ, a temple of the Spirit. (CCC 364)

There are days when Mam looks quite depressed. There is no recognition in her eyes and no reaction to conversation. She is loathe to make contact, even by hand. She lies there, as if alone on a desert island, lamenting her loss. Yesterday, thank God, was very different. The light shone in her eyes, there was a smile on her face, she answered some questions and even tried to start a conversation. She observed every person walking by her in the corridor and noticed that one lady had red hair.

When Alzheimer's disease limits human interaction, even the smallest sign of normality is a pearl of great price. The taken-for-granted ordinary things of every day become remarkable events, suffused with extraordinary vigour. It's as if the potter God of creation was saying to us: 'Don't be upset by the appearance of this pot, there's much more to it than meets the eye. It's still in my hands, and I'm able to shape it into a beautiful vase'.

> Or do you not know that your body is a temple of the Holy Spirit within you, which you have from God, and that you are not your own? For you were bought with a price; therefore glorify God in your body. (1 Corinthians 6:19-20)

> Man and woman have been created ... on the one hand, in perfect equality as human persons; on the other, in their respective beings as man and woman. (CCC 369)

On a ten-hour flight to Los Angeles, I managed to read *Pythagoras' Trousers*. This is a great book about the possible link between mathematical science, religion and sexual discrimination against women. The author, a trained scientist who noticed the absence of women from the hard sciences and also from positions of power in the Christian Churches, wondered might these facts be somehow connected.

Are women and men of equal dignity? Are women and men entitled to an equal share of the power positions in the world? Is visibility the same as reality? If God is beyond sex, being neither male nor female, but truly the creator of both women and men, how can God's world be whole and healthy unless all women and all men have their rightful place within it? Does God have favourites?

> So the LORD God caused a deep sleep to fall upon the man, and he slept; then he took one of his ribs and closed up its place with flesh. And the rib that the LORD God had taken from the man he made into a woman and brought her to the man. Then the man said, 'This at last is bone of my bones and flesh of my flesh; this one shall be called Woman, for out of Man this one was taken'. (Genesis 2:21-23)

> Sin is an abuse of the freedom that God gives to created persons so that they are capable of loving him and loving one another. (CCC 387)

The computer virus attacking the internet has been blocked, and everybody breathes a sigh of relief. We depend so much on technology today that when it comes under viral threat we feel bedevilled. The range of communication by internet is unbelievable. One can gain access to countless libraries and databases. One can find out about almost anything in the world. One can book next year's holiday or order a half-ton of cement. One can send emails to friends and relations, and just as easily to the Pope or President Bush.

The internet is a source of immense pleasure and enlightenment. But still there are begrudgers. Still there are those who want to tear down what human ingenuity has built up, to destroy what bright people have constructed, to annoy the innocent and to upset the sophisticated. Using the best in communications to block communications is a peculiarly sick joke. Is it further evidence of original sin?

> If, because of the one man's trespass, death exercised dominion through that one, much more surely will those who receive the abundance of grace and the free gift of righteousness exercise dominion in life through the one man, Jesus Christ. Therefore just as one man's trespass led to condemnation for all, so one man's act of righteousness leads to justification and life for all. For just as by the one man's disobedience the many were made sinners, so by the one man's obedience the many will be made righteous. (Romans 5:17-19)

> The doctrine of original sin is, so to speak, the 'reverse side' of the Good News that Jesus is the Saviour of all men, that all need salvation and that salvation is offered to all through Christ. (CCC 389)

More and more we discover how interconnected the world is. Remember 9/11 – the bombs in Manhattan killed thousands in a few hours, but the fallout continues throughout the world. Fewer people want to fly, so airlines go broke and people working in tourism lose income. Unemployment increases, and with it the accompanying lack of hope and lack of needed resources for family life.

If the whole world is a pond, the stones dropped on the surface produce ripples that run to the edges. Such is the contagion of sin and destruction. But good people, too, can have a powerful impact. Their work, inspired by the Spirit of God, is often unseen and unheralded. Usually it occurs way beneath the surface. But occasionally it gushes forth and becomes a visible fountain, a joy to watch, a disturber of surface calm, and a presage of hidden life still to emerge.

> Her husband Joseph, being a righteous man and unwilling to expose her to public disgrace, planned to dismiss her quietly. But just when he had resolved to do this, an angel of the Lord appeared to him in a dream and said, 'Joseph, son of David, do not be afraid to take Mary as your wife, for the child conceived in her is from the Holy Spirit. She will bear a son, and you are to name him Jesus, for he will save his people from their sins'. (Matthew 1:19-21)

> As a result of original sin, human nature is weakened in its powers, subject to ignorance, suffering and the domination of death, and inclined to sin (this inclination is called 'concupiscence'). (CCC 418)

The man was remarkably calm as he talked about the cluster bombs falling in the courtyard of his house. Neither he nor his wife was injured, but every single one of his six children were killed. He showed the photographs to the reporter one by one, as he called out their names. They are all gone – his wife sits disconsolate at the door, her face in shock, unable to comprehend the tragedy.

War statistics are cold and clinical; they merely add up the figures and give the total number of those killed and injured. They never evoke the hurt and pain of the individual people killed, or the grief and tears of those who remain behind to lament their passing. For ally or foe, the human tragedy of war is the same. Brothers and sisters have been destroyed, and some light has been quenched in the heart of humanity.

> Therefore, just as sin came into the world through one man, and death came through sin, and so death spread to all because all have sinned. (Romans 5:12)

I Believe in Jesus Christ, the Only Son of God

> Moved by the grace of the Holy Spirit and drawn by the Father, we believe in Jesus and confess: 'You are the Christ, the Son of the living God'. (CCC 424)

Reflecting on the meaning of myth, especially religious myth, we noticed how readily people today think that myth is something unreal, airy-fairy or childish. That, indeed, can be the first reaction of many people to the story of Adam and Eve. But myth, in the judgement of scholars, is a privileged imaginative way of gaining access to mystery. Myth is very real, very serious and very adult, even though we find it remarkably hard to talk about it in ordinary language.

The myth of Santa Claus now has a secular version, but once it had a firm religious base. St Nicholas, a bishop who was generous to poor people, became in turn Sint Klaes (in Dutch America) and then Santa Claus (in the Western world). The story of Santa Claus is a story of gifts to everybody and generosity towards all. This myth reveals at the heart of life a mysterious generosity (called God), whose Son Jesus is the truest, finest and perfect gift of all. Long live this myth!

> Now when Jesus came into the district of Caesarea Philippi, he asked his disciples, 'Who do people say that the Son of Man is?' And they said, 'Some say John the Baptist, but others Elijah, and still others Jeremiah or one of the prophets.' He said to them, 'But who do you say that I am?' Simon Peter answered, 'You are the Messiah, the Son of the living God.' (Matthew 16:13-16)

> Caesar is not 'the Lord'. 'The Church ... believes that the key, the centre and the purpose of the whole of man's history is to be found in its Lord and Master' (Gaudium et spes, 10#3). (CCC 450)

Clearly Jesus is making an impact, so they ask him a loaded question: 'Should we pay taxes to Rome?' If he says 'yes', the Pharisees can say he has betrayed the Jewish Nation. If he says 'no', the Herodians can say he doesn't recognise the Emperor. It's a clever trap. Jesus can't win. He calls for a 'denarius' and asks what is on the coin. They say, 'Caesar's head'. 'Well then', said Jesus, 'if you are clearly benefiting from Caesar's reign, you should pay your taxes to Rome'.

Jesus then adds something very special. He says that there are things in life far more important than politics and jobs and money. The most important thing for any human to do is to pay attention to God, to give praise and thanks to God. We can't pay money to God; God is outside the money economy. But God wants something even more precious from us than money; he wants our hearts and our love. All the great saints knew that fact of life, and lived it every day.

> The one who testifies to these things says, 'Surely I am coming soon'. Amen. Come, Lord Jesus! (Revelation 22:20)

> To be a Christian, one must believe that Jesus Christ is the Son of God. (CCC 454)

The Anglican Dean of Clonmacnoise, Andrew Furlong, was suspended from priestly duties for not believing in the Incarnation. Articles he wrote on the Church's website were removed. In a radio interview he spoke about the importance of free speech, and of the need to constantly explore the Christian message. He talked about Jesus as a Jewish prophet, and as an inspiring moral teacher, who unfortunately got it wrong regarding death and the end-time.

One could agree with much he said. But no mention of resurrection, no belief in incarnation and no conviction regarding Jesus as a saviour together suggest that Andrew has moved outside the Christian story. He offers a limited truth, but certainly not the whole truth about Jesus. Jesus was a Jew, Jesus was a prophet and Jesus taught people how to live well. But Jesus was the Word of God made flesh. The Father raised the dead Jesus from the dead. In his name our sins are forgiven.

> Who is the liar but the one who denies that Jesus is the Christ? This is the antichrist, the one who denies the Father and the Son. No one who denies the Son has the Father; everyone who confesses the Son has the Father also. (1 John 2:22)

> The only-begotten Son of God, wanting to make us sharers in his divinity, assumed our nature, so that he, made man, might make men gods. (CCC 460)

As I went out for Mass one morning, Michael told me I was the only priest who would read the Gospel text, the genealogy of Jesus. Why do I love this text, while others find it a burden? All I can say is that I have always been interested in knowing where people came from and who their ancestors were. To me it matters a lot to know who Jesus' people were, and when I read this passage every year it is a powerful reminder of the fact that he is like us in all things but sin.

To be truly human is to be born into a family and have pride in one's ancestors. How did Jesus remember King David, one of the highpoints of his ancestry? As a poor man who made it into the big time? As a king who lusted after Bathsheba, the wife of one of his soldiers? As a murderer who saw to it that Uriah (her husband) would be killed, so that he (David) could then take this beautiful wife for himself? Or did Jesus remember David as the man who repented and cast himself on the mercy of God, where he was forgiven all his sins and restored to God's grace?

> May grace and peace be yours in abundance in the knowledge of God and of Jesus our Lord. His divine power has given us everything needed for life and godliness, through the knowledge of him who called us by his own glory and goodness. Thus he has given us, through these things, his precious and very great promises, so that through them you may escape from the corruption that is in the world because of lust, and may become participants of the divine nature. (2 Peter 1:2-4)

> He became truly man while remaining truly God.
> Jesus Christ is true God and true man. (CCC 464)

The lecture was entitled 'Jesus' discernment of his vocation'. We were reminded that Jesus was like us in all things but sin, in other words, he was truly human. He experienced the struggle of every human being to work out what God wanted of him. From his mother he learnt he was very special. But neither the teachers of the Law in the Temple, nor the prophet John the Baptist in the desert could offer him full clarity about his mission. He knew the anguish of testing or temptation.

Mary, too, had to struggle in her relationship with Jesus. Though she always recognised he was unique, she could also imagine he was mad, and even once tried to stop him carrying out his teaching and healing mission. It took the experience of his resurrection to convert her into his disciple. Sinless Mary, just like her sinless son, had to learn the hard way the meaning of God's mysterious plan for the world. We can find in both of them an encouraging example, as we too seek to know the will of God for us.

> By this you know the Spirit of God: every spirit that confesses that Jesus Christ has come in the flesh is from God, and every spirit that does not confess Jesus is not from God. (1 John 4:2-3)

> [T]he Sacred Heart of Jesus, pierced by our sins and for our salvation, is quite rightly considered the chief sign and symbol of that ... love with which the divine Redeemer continually loves the eternal Father and all human beings without exception. (CCC 478)

John Eudes lived in the seventeenth century, at a time when Jansenism was rife in France. This strange form of Catholic spirituality was very negative in its assessment of human life, and preached a harsh God for a sinful and corrupt people. John Eudes, apart from founding a famous Missionary Congregation, also worked closely with Margaret Mary Alacoque to develop devotion to the Sacred Heart of Jesus and the Holy Heart of Mary.

'Heart' represents the passion of God for his creatures, who are of inestimable worth, but who also fall into sin and need to be rescued from its clutches. The cold, clinical, repressive theology of Jansen met its match in the warmth and joy of the twin devotions to Jesus and his mother. Many Catholics found support for living from these vibrant prayer traditions. The liturgical renewal of Vatican II never meant such devotions to be destroyed, but unfortunately they often were.

> But when they came to Jesus and saw that he was already dead, they did not break his legs. Instead, one of the soldiers pierced his side with a spear, and at once blood and water came out. (John 19:33-34)

> What the Catholic faith believes about Mary is based on what it believes about Christ, and what it teaches about Mary illumines in turn its faith in Christ. (CCC 487)

The feast of the birthday of Our Lady developed rather late in the Church, under the influence of the Holy Spirit at work in the lives of prayerful disciples of Christ. In a sense, this late development parallels the way the Church introduced the feast of Christmas much later than the feast of Easter. To rejoice in a birthday is something very human. Having done so for Jesus Christ, it was natural to do the same for Mary his mother.

It was only after Christians had long contemplated Christ's death and resurrection that they felt the need to invest so much devotional energy in celebrating the day of his birth. Likewise, after meditating on Mary's being specially chosen by God, and after acknowledging that she was the all-holy Mother of God, it made sense to rejoice in Mary's birth as a daughter of Israel.

> In the sixth month the angel Gabriel was sent by God to a town in Galilee called Nazareth, to a virgin engaged to a man whose name was Joseph, of the house of David. The virgin's name was Mary. And he came to her and said, 'Greetings, favoured one! The Lord is with you'. (Luke 1:26-28)

> In fact, the One whom [Mary] conceived as man by the Holy Spirit ... was none other than the Father's eternal Son, the second person of the Holy Trinity. Hence the Church confesses that Mary is truly 'Mother of God' (Theotokos). (CCC 495)

Elizabeth was long past childbearing age, and then one day she realised she was going to have a baby. To be without a child was then regarded as a great tragedy. Elizabeth had beseeched God to give her a child, but God had remained silent. She continued to pray, and then when she was beginning to lose all hope the unexpected happened: she found she was pregnant. She would have thought to herself, 'What a way for God to work?'

Mary was very different. She was unmarried, though Joseph wanted to marry her. Then he found she was pregnant. Since he knew it wasn't his child, he wondered could she have been unfaithful. Better to divorce her quietly so that nobody would think badly of her. Mary, however, knew a different story. She knew of an angel inviting her to become the mother of God's own Son. Her thoughts would have been, 'What a surprising God?'

> When Elizabeth heard Mary's greeting, the child leaped in her womb. And Elizabeth was filled with the Holy Spirit and exclaimed with a loud cry, 'Blessed are you among women, and blessed is the fruit of your womb. And why has this happened to me, that the mother of my Lord comes to me?' (Luke 1:41-43)

> Jesus was born in a humble stable, into a poor
> family. Simple shepherds were the first witnesses
> to this event. In this poverty heaven's glory was
> made manifest. (CCC 525)

The Palestinian people mourned the death of Yasser
Arafat. As I prayed for the repose of his soul, I thought
back to 2001 when he was not allowed to visit
Bethlehem on Christmas Day. Ever since he became the
supreme authority in Palestine (which includes the city
of Bethlehem), he had gone there to pray on Christmas
day. But there was so much dissatisfaction in Israeli
Government circles about his alleged softness on
terrorists that he was banned from making the journey.
In spite of his claim that he would go there on foot,
common sense and his general ill health kept him at
home on that solemn Christian feast.

A Muslim leader showing such regard for a major
Christian feast should not surprise us. Muslims respect
Jesus as a minor prophet. Muslims have great regard
also for Mary, the mother of Jesus. As a people who
pray five times a day, Muslims also respect the prayer
life of Christians, and for centuries Muslim authorities
in Palestine have allowed Christian Churches to survive
and Christian pilgrims to travel to the places associated
with Jesus.

> While they were there, the time came for her to
> deliver her child. And she gave birth to her
> firstborn son and wrapped him in bands of cloth,
> and laid him in a manger, because there was no
> place for them in the inn. (Luke 2:6-7)

> [The baptism of Jesus] is the manifestation ('Epiphany') of Jesus as Messiah of Israel and Son of God. (CCC 535)

'Paddy the Irishman, Paddy the Englishman and Paddy the Scotsman' – many good stories have three characters. The three gifts mentioned in the Gospel of the Epiphany translate very easily into three wise men (though the text never mentions three men). Another three is the linking together of the Epiphany, the Baptism of Christ and the Wedding Feast of Cana. A beautiful carol tells of these three as if they are all connected – and they are.

The link is 'revelation'. When the wise men from the east come to worship the child in the crib, the hidden mystery of God is being revealed to the pagan nations. At his baptism by John in the Jordan, the deepest mystery of Jesus – the fact that he is truly God's unique Son – is revealed to Israel. When water is changed into wine at Cana, Jesus Christ reveals the true face of God as generosity beyond compare, as grace beyond expectation.

> And when Jesus had been baptised, just as he came up from the water, suddenly the heavens were opened to him and he saw the Spirit of God descending like a dove and alighting on him. And a voice from heaven said, 'This is my Son, the Beloved, with whom I am well pleased'. (Matthew 3:16-17)

> The evangelists indicate the salvific meaning of this mysterious event [Jesus' temptations]: Jesus is the new Adam who remained faithful just where the first Adam had given in to temptation. (CCC 539)

Jesus was fully human, and so he felt the power of temptation. He felt its subtle attraction – how you are pulled in a direction your better self doesn't want to go. When he was tempted in the desert, Jesus experienced one of the deepest feelings that humans can have: your conscience says one thing, and the temptation says another. There is a great drama and the outcome is uncertain. Maybe you'll give in to temptation, but maybe not.

Though Jesus resisted temptation, he obviously felt its power. Whenever we feel tempted, it's good to remember the story of Jesus in the desert. It should encourage us to face our own temptations with courage, drawing inspiration from our brother Jesus. And even if we sometimes give in to temptation and fall into sin, then we can also remember that the name Jesus means 'saviour'. He became our brother to save us from our sins.

> And the Spirit immediately drove him out into the wilderness. He was in the wilderness forty days, tempted by Satan; and he was with the wild beasts; and the angels waited on him. (Mark 1:12-13)

> Everyone is called to enter the kingdom. (CCC 543)

A few years ago, in Vicar Street, John McGahern was talking to Myles Dungan of *Rattlebag*. Why does an author write a novel? The huge, attentive audience heard McGahern speaking from the heart: he writes novels because they enable him to reveal the beauty in ordinary living. He is ruthless in his editing; hundreds of pages and many characters were dropped before the new novel was published.

In the Kingdom of God, as preached by Jesus, there are no favourites. All are invited to join in the wedding feast, because all are equal in God's sight. The ordinary as well as the extraordinary, the commoner as well as the king, the less talented as well as the gifted, the normal as well as the special – all have equal standing in the sight of God, and all are equally treasured by the God of Jesus Christ.

> Go therefore and make disciples of all nations, baptising them in the name of the Father and of the Son and of the Holy Spirit, and teaching them to obey everything that I have commanded you. And remember, I am with you always, to the end of the age. (Matthew 28:19-20)

> Jesus' entry into Jerusalem manifests the coming of the kingdom that the Messiah-King, welcomed into his city by children and the humble of heart, is going to accomplish by the Passover of his Death and Resurrection. (CCC 570)

Remembering Jesus' triumphant entry into Jerusalem, we often contrast the excitement of Palm Sunday with the horrors of Good Friday. This is a good theme for Lenten reflection: how fickle we can be in regard to God and God's business. On one day we praise the Son of David; a few days later we crucify him. All humanity does today what a few people did on that momentous occasion.

However, there is another reason now for further reflection and lament. In spite of a Christian presence in Jerusalem for about two thousand years, it seems that Christians are leaving the city and its surroundings in such great numbers now that very soon there will only be buildings instead of believers to remind us of the story of Jesus. Jerusalem without Christians may sound impossible. Post-Christian North Africa should give us food for thought.

> Rejoice greatly, O daughter Zion! Shout aloud, O daughter Jerusalem! Lo, your king comes to you; triumphant and victorious is he, humble and riding on a donkey, on a colt, the foal of a donkey. (Zechariah 9:9)

> The Paschal mystery of Christ's cross and Resurrection stands at the centre of the Good News that the apostles, and the Church following them, are to proclaim to the world. (CCC 571)

On the front pages of many tabloid newspapers, the sins of the Catholic Church are publicly noted. The message is very simple: 'This Church is corrupt and very bad for you. If you had any sense you would join us in mocking it, and, if you continue to belong to it, you ought to drop your subscriptions immediately or avoid its gatherings like the plague'. For those readers who are not fully convinced of this rhetoric and who dare to go to Mass today, the Gospel message has a different tone.

It reminds us that the story of Jesus, the central theme of the church, is one of Good News to all nations. Of course there is widespread sin (was it ever any different?), but an even more powerful force is already at work in the hearts of people, calling upon them gently to 'give up their old sins', so that their hearts can be filled with care and compassion. When John pointed to Jesus and called him the one who would 'baptise with the Holy Spirit', this is what he meant.

> Nor was it to offer himself again and again, as the high priest enters the Holy Place year after year with blood that is not his own; for then he would have had to suffer again and again since the foundation of the world. But as it is, he has appeared once for all at the end of the age to remove sin by the sacrifice of himself. (Hebrews 9:25-26)

> The Jewish people and their spiritual leaders viewed Jesus as a rabbi ... Yet Jesus ... taught the people 'as one who had authority, and not as their scribes'. (CCC 581)

Respect is central to teaching. If teachers are to be good at their job they need self-respect as a start; but they must also be respectful of all their pupils, and of the world in general. Teaching is a moral activity: it makes major human demands on all the participants; its process should be life enhancing; and its outcomes should be valued by society. To be a teacher today is to carry many heavy loads, but to be a teacher of religion is a truly challenging task. It requires not just normal respect, but the more problematic respect for religious sensitivities.

We are fortunate, therefore, that we have in our sights a challenging role model. For Christians, Jesus is the religion teacher *par excellence*. What he taught was what he lived. What he did himself, what he thought himself, what he imagined himself was precisely what he expected from his disciples. He was a true teacher.

> Now when Jesus had finished saying these things, the crowds were astounded at his teaching, for he taught them as one having authority, and not as their scribes. (Matthew 7:28-29)

> The personal sin of the participants (Judas, the Sanhedrin, Pilate) is known to God alone. (CCC 597)

The Wednesday before Easter is called Spy Wednesday in memory of the treachery of Judas. When Judas, a trusted disciple of Jesus, became informer and sold his master for thirty pieces of silver, this was the prelude to the infamous kiss in the garden of Gethsemane. Judas broke all the rules of decency. The question must be posed: how did he fall from grace? After being specially chosen by Jesus to be a close companion, how could he hand his master over to his sworn enemies?

Was Judas fundamentally flawed? Hardly, or Jesus would never have invited him to share his life and ministry. Judas must have had a good 'head for money' and been generally a trustworthy man, or he would never have been put in charge of the common fund. Was it greed that changed him? When did he become a thief? When his early thieving was successful, was it easier to go further and long for even more money? Why is the love of money the root of all evil?

> When they came to the place that is called The Skull, they crucified Jesus there with the criminals, one on his right and one on his left. Then Jesus said, 'Father, forgive them; for they do not know what they are doing'. (Luke 23:33-34)

> The Church, following the apostles, teaches that Christ died for all men without exception: 'There is not, never has been, and never will be a single human being for whom Christ did not suffer' (Council of Quiercy, 853). (CCC 605)

Visiting a house recently, I saw on the wall a small cross made of turf from a bog in Connemara. It's modelled on a famous old stone Celtic cross. The most remarkable thing about this cross is the figure of Jesus. Instead of the twisted corpse hanging in agony that we see above most altars, there is a majestic figure who is in control and master of the situation, standing erect with two arms outstretched.

The earliest Christian artists never portrayed the agony of Jesus on the cross. Instead, they portrayed the cross as a throne of victory. Jesus was shown as a king on his throne, dressed in kingly robes and with a real crown on his head instead of a crown of thorns. What sort of thinking lies behind this kind of art? Perhaps the realisation that there was something kingly about the way Jesus laid down his life for humankind.

> What do you think? If a shepherd has a hundred sheep, and one of them has gone astray, does he not leave the ninety-nine on the mountains and go in search of the one that went astray? And if he finds it, truly I tell you, he rejoices over it more than over the ninety-nine that never went astray. So it is not the will of your Father in heaven that one of these little ones should be lost. (Matthew 18:12-14)

Jesus freely offered himself for our salvation. (CCC 621)

Maximilian Kolbe was a Franciscan priest who did something very noble in the concentration camp at Auschwitz. One of the inmates, who happened to be a married man, was condemned to death, but Kolbe offered to take his place in front of the firing line so that this man could be reunited with his wife and family. Kolbe gave up his own greatest treasure so that another human being might have life.

He was very brave to face a violent death without much preparation. He showed great character by giving his life, not for a friend (which would have made some sense), but simply for another human being. What could possibly have motivated him to give up everything in this generous manner? Perhaps it was his conviction that Jesus died young to save us, even though we are undeserving sinners.

> For this reason the Father loves me, because I lay down my life in order to take it up again. No one takes it from me, but I lay it down of my own accord. I have power to lay it down, and I have power to take it up again. I have received this command from my Father. (John 10:17-18)

'By the grace of God' Jesus tasted death 'for every one'. (CCC 624)

During our parish's prayer service for those involved in the Asian tsunami, a phrase in one of the prayers caught my attention. Focussing on those who had been bereaved, it asked, among other things, that they could begin to find some meaning in this tragedy. This issue, the question of trying to make some sense out of such horror, had already been raised on TV shows and in the newspapers: how can religious people continue to believe in a good God?

At that moment, we were facing the crucifix on the back wall of our church, and it began to dawn on me that it is only in gazing on that horror that one can begin to understand any human tragedy. Calvary was the epitome of disaster: the innocent Son of God wiped out by the evil of real people. Since that tragic day, the Son of God knows disaster, not just as an observer, but from the depths of his own human heart. God knows grief from within. God feels for our pain.

[B]ut we do see Jesus, who for a little while was made lower than the angels, now crowned with glory and honour because of the suffering of death, so that by the grace of God he might taste death for everyone. (Hebrews 2:9)

> In his risen body he passes from the state of death to another life beyond time and space. (CCC 646)

As long as I have been going down to west Kerry, I have loved the beautiful sandy Coumeenole Beach, the most westerly in mainland Ireland, overlooking the Blaskets and facing towards America. I was horrified one day to see that it had been totally covered in rocks. On close inspection, I found that these did not come from the majestic cliffs above the beach; given their smooth surface, they must have come from the sea.

Speaking to some local people about this disaster, I discovered that they were less worried than I: 'In a while the sea will undo its work and the sand will reappear'. I hoped they were right. I felt like the disciples of Jesus: upset and terrified at his demise. But then, to their amazement, the power of God's Spirit raised him from the dead, and they met one who was so transformed they barely recognised him.

> So it is with the resurrection of the dead. What is sown is perishable, what is raised is imperishable. It is sown in dishonour, it is raised in glory. It is sown in weakness, it is raised in power. It is sown a physical body, it is raised a spiritual body. If there is a physical body, there is also a spiritual body. (1 Corinthians 15:42-44)

> The Paschal mystery has two aspects: by his death,
> Christ liberates us from sin; by his Resurrection,
> he opens for us the way to a new life. (CCC 654)

Letting go is very difficult, but it is the only way into new life. This was the theme of Michael Drumm's preaching at a Mass for Pat Matthew's husband in our oratory. Since our first letting go, out of our mother's womb into the world of family life, all of life follows this pattern. We all have to let go of childhood so that we can grow up into full maturity. Parents must let their children go so that they can become themselves. Children have to let their parents go in death.

We must let go of jobs when health fails, or economies falter, or retirement beckons. Finally, we must all let go of our own life, the greatest treasure we know, so that we can pass through death to eternal life with God. Christians see in the death and resurrection of Jesus what we call the Paschal Mystery, the deepest meaning of human life. Letting go allows God to offer us a new fullness of life.

> But God, who is rich in mercy, out of the great love
> with which he loved us even when we were dead
> through our trespasses, made us alive together with
> Christ – by grace you have been saved – and raised us
> up with him and seated us with him in the heavenly
> places in Christ Jesus, so that in the ages to come he
> might show the immeasurable riches of his grace in
> kindness toward us in Christ Jesus. (Ephesians 2:4-7)

> Jesus Christ, the head of the Church, precedes us into the Father's glorious kingdom so that we, the members of his body, may live in the hope of one day being with him for ever. (CCC 666)

Ascension Thursday now happens on a Sunday. This reflects the fact that few people have been attending Mass on the Thursday feast, and it makes sense to move the feast to Sunday when most people still go to church. This is a feast of hope. The fact that someone like us in all things but sin should now be fully at one with the Father is worth pondering upon. His arrival back home with the Father is good news for us – where he has gone we can now hope to go.

But why do we benefit from his safe arrival home? This is only possible because we are an integral part of his body. Since baptism we have been members of his body, he being the head. The head and members together form the extended body of Christ. Where the head has gone, the body is meant to go. We have a place in store for us, as body members of Christ, provided we remain in him through grace.

> In my Father's house there are many dwelling places. If it were not so, would I have told you that I go to prepare a place for you? And if I go and prepare a place for you, I will come again and will take you to myself, so that where I am, there you may be also. (John 12:2-3)

> On the Last Day Jesus will say: 'Truly I say to you, as you did it to one of the least of these my brethren, you did it to me'. (CCC 678)

The Housing and Community Services Department of Dublin City Council has statutory responsibility for looking after homeless people in Dublin. To complement this work, there are also many voluntary organisations that care for the homeless. The Simon Community and Focus Ireland, St Vincent de Paul, the Salvation Army and Crosscare are the best known. In spite of the energy and compassion of all these service providers, the number of homeless people continues to grow.

How does one become homeless today, in a wealthy Ireland with many excellent services on offer? Some homeless people are on the street because of family breakdown, sexual abuse, alcoholism, or psychological trauma. Others may be new arrivals to the country, still waiting for jobs and proper accommodation. An increasing number of homeless people are very young, and many have had a bad experience with drugs. Whenever we look after people on the margins, we are caring for Jesus in the least of his sisters and brothers.

> Then they also will answer, 'Lord, when was it that we saw you hungry or thirsty or a stranger or naked or sick or in prison, and did not take care of you?' Then he will answer them, 'Truly I tell you, just as you did not do it to one of the least of these, you did not do it to me'. (Matthew 25:44-45)

I Believe in the Holy Spirit

> The term 'Spirit' translates the Hebrew word
> *ruah*, which, in its primary sense, means breath,
> air, wind. (CCC 691)

The summer heat arrives and it reaches thirty plus each day. Without air-conditioning it would be almost impossible to sleep at night. During the day one is very careful by the pool, conscious of the power of the naked sun. Umbrellas are essential for survival. Some holidaymakers take risks and spend too long under the midday sun, or jump and swim in the pool. Red bodies remind one of the effects of the sun on unprepared flesh.

Then the gentle breeze begins to move. Without any advance warning, it begins to rustle through the palm-trees. The umbrellas dance a jig and the air has a freshness that pleases. Was it like this one Sunday long ago when a frightened group of Jews gathered together out of fear of attack? Were they unable to bear the heat of the day? Did they need the soothing balm of God's Holy Spirit?

> What is born of the flesh is flesh, and what is born
> of the Spirit is spirit. Do not be astonished that I
> said to you, 'You must be born from above.' The
> wind blows where it chooses, and you hear the
> sound of it, but you do not know where it comes
> from or where it goes. So it is with everyone who
> is born of the Spirit. (John 3:6-8)

Fire symbolises the transforming energy of the
Holy Spirit's actions. (CCC 696)

A huge fire blazed in a yard behind the flats in the fruit-
market area of Dublin. As fireworks exploded in the
night sky, a sizeable group of people watched from a
safe distance across the road. Nobody had called them
out, they just came, willing to stand and watch. I
thought of our tiny Easter fires in small containers at the
back of the church, making hardly enough light to read
by. Why do we find it so hard to do things well, and put
on a memorable performance?

St Patrick knew the story of Moses on Mount Sinai and
how God appeared to him in a burning bush. He knew
that the Lord Jesus once said he had come to cast fire
upon the earth and wished that it was already kindled.
And he knew by heart the account of Pentecost and the
Spirit coming down on the believers in tongues of fire.
So, when Patrick noticed the druids' fire on the Hill of
Slane, he joined the people in their religious ritual. He
told them that day about the light of the world.

John answered all of them by saying, 'I baptise you
with water; but one who is more powerful than I is
coming; I am not worthy to untie the thong of his
sandals. He will baptise you with the Holy Spirit
and fire'. (Luke 3:16)

> The Word of God and his Breath are at the origin of the being and life of every creature. (CCC 703)

When I searched in Google for some information on SARS (Severe Acute Respiratory Syndrome) at the time of the outbreak, I discovered that there were over four hundred pages devoted to the topic. It was hard to believe that such a new health scare could already be so well documented. The world is becoming more and more like a global village. My hope for epidemics of this kind is that people treat each other as friendly neighbours, rather than resisting each other as foreign bodies.

With polluted lungs, we can pollute the air for others; we can transfer to them the source of the illness that may cause death. SARS may help us to recognise how central to life two healthy lungs are. Without pure air we are dead. Of course, in religious experience, the same pattern arises. We who have been graced with the outpouring of God's Holy Spirit (God's living breath) can, in our own turn, breathe on others and share with them the life power that nourishes our deepest spirit.

> By the word of the LORD the heavens were made, and all their host by the breath of his mouth. (Psalms 33:6)

> John the Baptist is 'more than a prophet'. In him, the Holy Spirit concludes his speaking through the prophets. John completes the cycle of prophets begun by Elijah. (CCC 719)

The Gospel readings at Mass recently talked about John the Baptist and Jesus of Nazareth. While both men were dedicated to the things of God, they each had very different styles. John was an ascetic, who stayed in the desert away from most human contact. Jesus, on the other hand, mixed with all sorts of people and was known as a party-goer who liked his wine. Each lifestyle has its own strengths and weaknesses.

In spite of these lifestyle differences, both John and Jesus agreed on many issues. They both recognised that people in general are sinners who need to turn back to God and be reconciled. They both felt the wrath of the religious leaders who objected to their prophetic statements, and who had both of them killed for their dedication to the truth. The early disciples of Jesus knew that Jesus had once followed after John – obviously because he respected him.

> What then did you go out to see? A prophet? Yes, I tell you, and more than a prophet. This is the one about whom it is written, 'See, I am sending my messenger ahead of you, who will prepare your way before you.' I tell you, among those born of women no one is greater than John; yet the least in the kingdom of God is greater than he. (Luke 7:26-28)

> Mary is acclaimed and represented in the liturgy as the 'Seat of Wisdom'. (CCC 721)

During his homily at our recent Graduation Mass, Gareth told us about a visit to Derry and how he noticed, above the entrance into a school, three very significant words: imagination, creativity and learning. From this he deduced that learning, the business of schools, comes usually at the end of a long journey. Learning may involve gathering information, it may also help to generate understanding, but its greatest achievement is wisdom.

Rooted in the imagination and built on creative activity, true learning is a treasure beyond price. The Mater Dei Institute of Education is dedicated to Mary, whom Catholic tradition calls *Sedes Sapientiae* (Seat of Wisdom). The students who spend four years preparing to become teachers of religion and an arts subject read, reflect, listen, debate, write and practise teaching skills. They learn a lot, they become very skilful at their profession, but the most important aspect of their education is the wisdom to which they all aspire.

> Wisdom speaks her own praises, in the midst of her people she glories in herself. She opens her mouth in the assembly of the Most High, she glories in herself in the presence of the Mighty One. (*NJB*, Sirach 24:1-2)

> The entire mission of the Son and the Holy Spirit, in the fullness of time, is contained in this: that the Son is the one anointed by the Father's Spirit since his Incarnation – Jesus is the Christ, the Messiah. (CCC 727)

If we summarise the Gospel of Luke (Luke 1:1-14, 4:14-21), it might sound something like this: 'People of Nazareth, all that your forefathers were looking forward to, poor people hearing good news, people in slavery being set free, blind people being able to see – in short, the beginning of the reign of God – all this is starting now. And it is I who am going to do all these things. I, one of your own townsmen. I, in fact, am the promised one you have all been waiting for'.

I'm sure the people of Nazareth, upon hearing these words, must have received quite a shock, for it is a shocking claim to make. But the same claim is made in every church every time people gather to celebrate Mass: 'Here in our midst is the promised one, speaking to us and giving himself to us as food for our life'. Surely that's a very good reason for coming to Mass on a Sunday – to listen to this good news and to thank God for sending Jesus to tell it.

> And I will ask the Father, and he will give you another Advocate, to be with you forever. This is the Spirit of truth, whom the world cannot receive, because it neither sees him nor knows him. You know him, because he abides with you, and he will be in you. (John 14:16-17)

> The mission of Christ and the Holy Spirit is brought to completion in the Church, which is the Body of Christ and the Temple of the Holy Spirit. (CCC 737)

Saul of Tarsus hated the early followers of Jesus. He gloated publicly over the stoning to death of Stephen by an enraged mob that had accused him of blasphemy. As a true son of the Jewish Law, Saul considered that he was being faithful to the God of Israel by persecuting the followers of Jesus. On his way to Damascus, in the furtherance of his 'holy war', the light of the Risen Christ shone around him and knocked him to the ground.

He was in turmoil. He realised that in attacking the followers he was attacking their Master. This perception of the vital bond between Jesus, raised from the dead, and the body of his faithful disciples was what converted Saul. Later on, as Paul (whose name change reflected a change of lifestyle), he spoke about the Church as the Body of Christ and its corporate members as temples of the Holy Spirit. Apart from Jesus himself, it is doubtful if anybody else played such a major part in shaping the Christian family's understanding of itself.

> Or do you not know that your body is a temple of the Holy Spirit within you, which you have from God, and that you are not your own? For you were bought with a price; therefore glorify God in your body. (1 Corinthians 6:19-20)

> In the Church, God is 'calling together' his people
> from all the ends of the earth. (CCC 751)

From the roof of the Ecumenical Institute in Tantur,
looking west one can see both Gilo (a modern Jewish
settlement) and Beit Jala (a traditional Arab town, with
a 90 per cent Christian population). From their lofty
perches, they eye one another across a small valley. In
response to shooting from Beit Jala, the Israeli army
shelled the Arab houses closest to Gilo. The Latin
Patriarch of Jerusalem appealed for a halt to the
shelling, and asked that at least the family homes be
spared: 'If you must shell buildings', he said, 'shell our
churches.'

The Christian presence in the Holy Land is under
serious threat. Even the frequent pilgrimages by
westerners are of dubious value. These often limit
themselves to viewing old ruins and old churches. The
presence of 'living stones' (people who have been
Christian for two thousand years) is seldom noted or
valued. While buildings are important, their value
derives from the people they house. While churches are
treasures, it is the church (the people) that really counts.

> You have heard, no doubt, of my earlier life in
> Judaism. I was violently persecuting the church of
> God and was trying to destroy it. (Galatians 1:13)

> The eternal Father ... created the whole universe, and chose to raise up men to share in his own divine life (Lumen Gentium, 2). (CCC 759)

During a tutorial on religious language, we explored a wide range of images commonly used for God. We recalled the phrase, 'I have raised you up on eagles' wings', and wondered about this image of God as an eagle. For Jews, who knew eagles, this image must have spoken to the heart. For modern Americans, whose national icon is the bald eagle, this kind of God-talk probably works very well. However, many people think of eagles only as birds of prey, so what are we to do?

One way around this problem is to emphasise instead the majesty of the eagle. We need to imagine it soaring up high, where it spots the plight of its little offspring below. We then follow the eagle swooping down to earth, and notice how the return flight supports the one borne aloft, while rescuing it from danger and transforming it into something wonderful. This is what God does for us poor humans.

> Now when Jesus came into the district of Caesarea Philippi, he asked his disciples, 'Who do people say that the Son of Man is?' And they said, 'Some say John the Baptist, but others Elijah, and still others Jeremiah or one of the prophets.' He said to them, 'But who do you say that I am?' Simon Peter answered, 'You are the Messiah, the Son of the living God.' (Matthew 16:13-16)

> The whole People of God participates in these three offices of Christ [priest, prophet and king] and bears the responsibilities for mission and service that flow from them. (CCC 783)

There has been much talk recently about the new parish priests in Dublin. June is the usual month for the changes to be announced, but what makes matters very interesting this time is the news that the average age of Dublin priests is now sixty-five. When I first heard this, I could hardly believe it. I have regarded myself as middle-aged since I turned thirty-five, but it turns out that I am actually a young priest, well below the average age!

The care of Dublin's parishes cannot be confined to the increasingly older cohort of ordained ministers. But maybe that is a good thing; maybe the community will learn at last that Baptism is the basic sacrament of mission. Now that more and more people are retiring in their fifties, perhaps they will at last be free to take on real responsibility for the management and leadership of parish communities. The era of the Parish Pastoral Council is upon us.

> John to the seven churches that are in Asia: Grace to you and peace from him who is and who was and who is to come, and from the seven spirits who are before his throne, and from Jesus Christ, the faithful witness, the firstborn of the dead, and the ruler of the kings of the earth. To him who loves us and freed us from our sins by his blood, and made us to be a kingdom, priests serving his God and Father, to him be glory and dominion forever and ever. Amen. (Revelation 1:4-6)

> The unity of Christ and the Church, head and members of one Body, also implies the distinction of the two within a personal relationship. This aspect is often expressed by the image of bridegroom and bride. (CCC 796)

Gaelic Ireland regularly sang about the Irish Nation as *Caitlín ní hUallacháin*, or some other such woman of great charm and beauty. At our recent Mass before graduation, in the redecorated Clonliffe College church, the tune played after Communion was another old Irish air, *An Chúilfhionn*, 'the fair one'. Some may have thought such a secular love song, in praise of a beautiful girlfriend, was out of place in a solemn liturgy.

However, there is a very long tradition of doing precisely that. What else is the *Song of Songs* but an unashamedly romantic poem, celebrating human passionate love, which the Jewish people have incorporated into their Sacred Scriptures? Both human and divine love grow from the same soil. God's dealings with God's people can be compared to the love between husband and wife. Christ's relationship with the Church is that of bridegroom and bride.

> Jesus said to them, 'The wedding guests cannot fast while the bridegroom is with them, can they? As long as they have the bridegroom with them, they cannot fast. The days will come when the bridegroom is taken away from them, and then they will fast on that day'. (Mark 2:19-20)

> It is the Holy Spirit ... who brings about that wonderful communion of the faithful and joins them together so intimately in Christ. (CCC 813)

In Dublin's North Inner City Deanery, the ten parishes are slowly learning to work together. Each year members of the parish teams go away for a few days to pray, reflect and relax together in order to develop richer contacts and deeper friendships, out of which may grow a more coordinated witness to the Gospel in the heart of the city. One result of our going away was the decision to have a social gathering each November in the Pro-Cathedral.

The food and drink are of high quality, and most of those invited make an effort to be present. Clergy and parish sisters mingle with lay folk and the Archbishop. It's a very valuable experience of communion. The hope is that more and more people in these ten parishes will experience such moments of communion, for the heart of God is communion, and God's will for all is that they may share in that inner life.

> I therefore, the prisoner in the Lord, beg you to lead a life worthy of the calling to which you have been called, with all humility and gentleness, with patience, bearing with one another in love, making every effort to maintain the unity of the Spirit in the bond of peace. (Ephesians 4:1-3)

> All who have been justified by faith in Baptism are incorporated into Christ; they therefore have a right to be called Christians, and with good reason are accepted as brothers in the Lord by the children of the Catholic Church. (CCC 818)

Reading the memoirs of Hans Kung, one of the most controversial theologians in recent years, I have enjoyed his account of student life in Rome and Paris (two cities where I was privileged to study, though after he had passed through). The book is entitled, *My Struggle for Freedom*, and the text explores in a variety of ways the strange but essential link between the Gospel and freedom.

Kung was a theological expert at the Second Vatican Council, and his writings before the Council proposed many precise areas for reform in the Catholic Church, the majority of which have by now been implemented. One major task still remains: the unity of the Christian family, the need for ecumenical outreach and humble repentance from every Christian ecclesial community. We are still a long way from realising the dream of Jesus, 'that they all may be one'.

> I ask not only on behalf of these, but also on behalf of those who will believe in me through their word, that they may all be one. As you, Father, are in me and I am in you, may they also be in us, so that the world may believe that you have sent me. The glory that you have given me I have given them, so that they may be one, as we are one, I in them and you in me, that they may become completely one, so that the world may know that you have sent me and have loved them even as you have loved me. (John 17:20-23)

By canonising some of the faithful, i.e. by solemnly proclaiming that they practised heroic virtue and lived in fidelity to God's grace, the Church recognises the power of the Spirit of holiness within her, and sustains the hope of believers by proposing the saints to them as models and intercessors. (CCC 828)

July 23 is the feast of St Bridget of Sweden. She was a noblewoman who lived in the fourteenth century. She married young and raised a large family. After the death of her husband, she devoted herself to a life of prayer. She also founded an order of nuns called the Bridgettines. After a pilgrimage to the Holy Land, she settled in Rome. She was canonised very shortly after her death and was named Patron of Europe in 2000.

What makes a person a saint? A life marked by outstanding virtue. Why are some people singled out for canonisation? To encourage everybody alive that it is possible, with God's help, to live an outstandingly loving, faithful and hopeful life. What can we learn from the lives of holy people? They share our humanity. We can ask God for the Holy Spirit poured out upon them, and God will surely pour the same Spirit on us, so that we too can live like them – in the love of God and neighbour.

But Ananias answered, 'Lord, I have heard from many about this man, how much evil he has done to your saints in Jerusalem; and here he has authority from the chief priests to bind all who invoke your name'. (Acts 9:13-14)

> The Church is catholic in a double sense: First, the Church is catholic because ... in her subsists the fullness of Christ's body united with its head ... Secondly, the Church is catholic because she has been sent out by Christ on a mission to the whole of the human race. (CCC 830-831)

Since 1999, most of the young men training to become priests for Dublin have been studying in St Patrick's College, Maynooth. It has always been a tradition in Dublin to welcome applicants from all over Ireland, and many eminent Dublin priests were not originally from Dublin. But one of the present Dublin clerical students in Maynooth comes from Ho Chi Minh City. I think this is a new occurrence; the Vietnamese community is still small in Dublin.

The Church is 'Catholic' in different senses. An obvious meaning of the term is 'universal'; there are communities of Catholics all over the world. Though they differ in human culture, they are one in faith and hope and love. Sometimes the cultural differences have been bad for the life of faith, but often the faith has been nourished in a foreign land by a stranger inspired by the love of God.

> And Jesus came and said to them, 'All authority in heaven and on earth has been given to me. Go therefore and make disciples of all nations, baptising them in the name of the Father and of the Son and of the Holy Spirit, and teaching them to obey everything that I have commanded you. And remember, I am with you always, to the end of the age'. (Matthew 28:18-20)

> The Catholic Church recognises in other religions that search, among shadows and images, for the God who is unknown yet near since he gives life and breath and all things, and wants all men to be saved. (CCC 843)

The centre of Bangkok contains the Royal Palace and numerous temples. Under a blue sky, the colours of the religious buildings are stunning: golden stupas and golden devils, with burnt sienna rooftops enclosed in white and green borders. There are Buddha statues in every conceivable position. People wander in and out quite informally, and some stop to light incense and pray briefly with downcast eyes.

The impact is immense. Here is a beautiful work of art to honour the great Lord Buddha. He was born rich and powerful in India, two thousand five hundred years ago. Upset by the poverty of most people, he sought a way out of suffering which led him to enlightenment. His millions of followers today try to walk his path of meditation, and by overcoming human desire they hope to reach the peace of Nirvana.

> For what can be known about God is plain to them, because God has shown it to them. Ever since the creation of the world his eternal power and divine nature, invisible though they are, have been understood and seen through the things he has made. So they are without excuse; for though they knew God, they did not honour him as God or give thanks to him, but they became futile in their thinking, and their senseless minds were darkened. (Romans 1:19-21)

> [T]he Church, in obedience to the command of her founder and because it is demanded by her own essential universality, strives to preach the Gospel to all men. (CCC 849)

Today we rejoice in all the people who have given up so much to go abroad on the foreign missions. They have been inspired by the life of Jesus and have gone to the ends of the earth to tell people his story, and to spread the Gospel message of Jesus' life, death and resurrection. The story and message of Jesus is a story full of hope and good news. Missionaries are hopeful people so caught up in this good news that they simply cannot wait to share it with everybody else.

But all of us at home are also called to be missionaries. We are meant to be part of the same mission on the home front. How else can people around us learn the story of Jesus unless they see it coming alive in our lives? We are supposed to be the light of the world. When people meet us and notice how we live, they ought to be able to catch a glimpse of the life of Jesus simply by observing our lifestyle. We baptised disciples are all called to make his face shine on earth forever.

> This is right and is acceptable in the sight of God our Saviour, who desires everyone to be saved and to come to the knowledge of the truth. For there is one God; there is also one mediator between God and humankind, Christ Jesus, himself human, who gave himself a ransom for all – this was attested at the right time. (1 Timothy 2:3-6)

> The Church is apostolic because ... she was and remains built on 'the foundation of the apostles', the witnesses chosen and sent on mission by Christ himself. (CCC 857)

John was a fisherman from Galilee, a son of Zebedee and a brother of James. He was called by Jesus to leave all and follow him. He became one of his most intimate disciples and was later appointed one of the twelve apostles. Tradition identifies him as the fourth evangelist, the so-called 'theologian' or 'divine'. Another tradition identifies him as the 'disciple whom Jesus loved' and places him at the foot of the cross, where Jesus commends his mother, Mary, to his care.

As an apostle, John had known Jesus during his public ministry and had met the risen Lord after his resurrection. In the power of this faith, John spent his life proclaiming that Jesus was the Messiah, the Christ of God, sent to forgive the sins of the whole world. As an evangelist (or perhaps the leader of an evangelising community), John saw to it that the good news was preserved in writing for all future generations of the Christian faithful who, listening to it, would grow into firm belief.

> So then you are no longer strangers and aliens, but you are citizens with the saints and also members of the household of God, built upon the foundation of the apostles and prophets, with Christ Jesus himself as the cornerstone. In him the whole structure is joined together and grows into a holy temple in the Lord; in whom you also are built together spiritually into a dwelling place for God. (Ephesians 2:19-22)

> Just as 'by the Lord's institution, St Peter and the rest of the apostles constitute a single apostolic college, so in like fashion the Roman Pontiff, Peter's successor, and the bishops, the successors of the apostles, are related with and united to one another'. (CCC 880)

The Ha'penny Bridge was repaired and painted an off white colour. It connects the two sides of the centre of Dublin city, allowing us Northerners access to Temple Bar with its exotic bars, shops and restaurants. Though not a stone bridge like most of its companions, it has a certain quiet elegance. It is good to have such a charming bridge, especially because the euro notes display bridges of no special charm or style.

Bridges foster commerce, and they also create political bonds. Bridge-building is a challenge in a divided world. When the early popes searched for images to capture their ministry, they called themselves *Pontifex Maximus* ('the supreme builder of bridges', a title once given to the Emperor). The Pope, as Pontiff, bridges the gap between God and the world, bringing God's Word of hope to people and raising their words of petition to God.

> And when day came, he called his disciples and chose twelve of them, whom he also named apostles: Simon, whom he named Peter, and his brother Andrew, and James, and John, and Philip, and Bartholomew, and Matthew, and Thomas, and James son of Alphaeus, and Simon, who was called the Zealot, and Judas son of James, and Judas Iscariot, who became a traitor. (Luke 6:13-16)

> Bishops, with priests as co-workers, have as their first task 'to preach the Gospel of God to all men', in keeping with the Lord's command. (CCC 888)

A bishop, late for an appointment with the Pope in the Vatican, was passing through the arcade beside the Bronze Doors when suddenly he saw a beggar. To his amazement, he recognised the face of a fellow priest, who years earlier had left the priesthood. Not wanting to delay, he gave him some coins and promised to talk with him later. Then he went to his meeting, greeted his fellow bishops, excused himself to the Pope for being delayed and explained the circumstances.

Then said the Pope: 'Go back down now and invite him in here for lunch'. The bishop did as he was told, brought up the beggar and all ate and drank together. After lunch, the Pope invited the beggar to hear his confession. The bishops were all visibly moved by the strange turn of events and were unable to debate the issues they had gathered to discuss. They had just witnessed a powerful proclamation of the Gospel.

> And he said to them, 'Go into all the world and proclaim the good news to the whole creation. The one who believes and is baptised will be saved; but the one who does not believe will be condemned'. (Mark 16:15-16)

> [The bishop] should not refuse to listen to his subjects whose welfare he promotes as his very own children. (CCC 896)

Should we have a synod? This is a question Dublin priests were asked to reflect on one day. In very pleasant surroundings in Malahide, and in a morning punctuated with psalms and other prayers, we were told about the major pastoral issues confronting Dublin. Afterwards, we heard about the workings of a synod, and finally we heard of the experience of a Diocesan Synod in Rome during the period 1986-1993.

The major reservations mentioned in the feedback were as follows: will it only be a talking shop, unable to advance genuine renewal? Will the entire People of God in Dublin really be consulted? And, if so, how? Does the Cardinal really want to call a synod? And, if it starts, could it die when he retires? Nearly 90 per cent of the priests said they favoured holding a synod in the immediate future.

> Now as an elder myself and a witness of the sufferings of Christ, as well as one who shares in the glory to be revealed, I exhort the elders among you to tend the flock of God that is in your charge, exercising the oversight, not under compulsion but willingly, as God would have you do it – not for sordid gain but eagerly. Do not lord it over those in your charge, but be examples to the flock. (1 Peter 5:1-3)

> Lay people also fulfil their prophetic mission by evangelisation, 'that is, the proclamation of Christ by word and the testimony of life'. (CCC 905)

The advertisements for *Power to Change*, 'an all-Ireland media and training initiative, seeking to encourage and equip ordinary Christians to share their faith' (www.share.powertochange.ie), cannot be broadcast over the national airwaves in Ireland. The courts have decided such advertising would be illegal. Though the Irish State 'shall respect and honour religion', the broadcasting law dictates that religion may not pay to display.

Some people are very upset by this, because no legal ban is placed on ads for cigarettes or alcohol, and little control is exercised on ads that subtly encourage sexual promiscuity or try to glamorise violence. Whatever the rights and wrongs of this interpretation of the law, there is a more worrying aspect to it. Why are the four main Churches, who together support *Power to Change*, unable to adequately fund the people who do the hard work of fostering the faith of Ireland's adults?

> Stand therefore, and fasten the belt of truth around your waist, and put on the breastplate of righteousness. As shoes for your feet put on whatever will make you ready to proclaim the gospel of peace. (Ephesians 6:14-15)

> Different religious families have come into existence
> in which spiritual resources are multiplied for the
> progress in holiness of their members and for the
> good of the entire Body of Christ. (CCC 917)

Members of the Dublin North Inner City Deanery were
away discussing Deanery business close to Carrickmacross,
and took the afternoon off to visit a monastery nearby.
This was New Mellifont, near the village of Collon in Co.
Louth. The Cistercians live there now, as once their
predecessors did a few miles away in a building long since
destroyed. During Mass, Adrian prayed for his parents
who had married there over fifty years ago and were still
living nearby.

It was a day to remember the past and to rejoice in our
Christian heritage. The monks work a beautiful farm and
gather together often each day to pray. They welcome
anybody who is happy to come away for a peaceful
moment of reflection. A teenager we met told us he was in
his sixth year at school in Gonzaga College in Dublin, and
his class were in the monastery for a short retreat. The old
monks and the young students seemed to get on very well
together.

> But he said to them, 'Not everyone can accept this
> teaching, but only those to whom it is given. For
> there are eunuchs who have been so from birth,
> and there are eunuchs who have been
> made eunuchs by others, and there are eunuchs
> who have made themselves eunuchs for the sake of
> the kingdom of heaven. Let anyone accept this
> who can'. (Matthew 19:11-12)

Moreover, 'since members of institutes of consecrated life dedicate themselves through their consecration to the service of the Church they are obliged in a special manner to engage in missionary work, in accord with the character of the institute' (Code of Canon Law, can. 783). (CCC 931)

A bishop in southern Sudan heard about the educational work of the Irish Loreto sisters and asked them to send some sisters to his troubled land. The long, drawn out civil war, the ethnic cleansing and drought and famine – all focussed briefly on Darfur – have kept Sudan in the eyes of the world. Some brave Irish women have left the comforts of home in order to walk with the poor, bereaved and displaced people of central Africa.

When we think of Africa, we automatically think of Irish missionaries going there to spread the Gospel. The large numbers are often cited and celebrated as a measure of our nation's rich Christian spirit. However, these statistics may hide the fact that each missionary is an individual, with fears and aspirations, gifts and prejudices. Each of the sisters that went abroad is to be complimented for showing the courage to give her life for the sake of others.

When Jesus saw the crowds, he went up the mountain; and after he sat down, his disciples came to him. Then he began to speak, and taught them, saying: 'Blessed are the poor in spirit, for theirs is the kingdom of heaven'. (Matthew 5:1-3)

> The life consecrated to God is characterised by the public profession of the evangelical counsels of poverty, chastity and obedience, in a stable state of life recognised by the Church. (CCC 944)

St Vincent de Paul is the major inspiration for a charitable society, composed of lay Catholics and dedicated to caring for poor people. He also founded two religious congregations: for sisters, the Daughters of Charity; and, for priests, the Congregation of the Mission (also called the Vincentians).

The word 'religious' is very interesting. When used today in Catholic circles it often refers to people who, inspired by the charism of a holy founder, live together in communities governed by vows of poverty, chastity and obedience. The two congregations founded by Vincent consist of precisely such 'religious' people. But the charitable society, open to lay Catholics, would rarely be classified as 'religious'. One wonders why this is so. Surely the work of caring for the poor is as much a part of 'religious life' as is the vowed life of sisters and priests?

> Through the testing of this ministry you glorify God by your obedience to the confession of the gospel of Christ and by the generosity of your sharing with them and with all others, while they long for you and pray for you because of the surpassing grace of God that he has given you. (2 Corinthians 9:13-14)

> The term 'communion of saints' refers also to the 'communion of holy persons' ('sancti') in Christ who 'died for all', so that what each one does or suffers in and for Christ bears fruit for all. (CCC 961)

Talking about the Communion of Saints in class, I noticed how reluctant the students were to apply the title 'saint' to themselves. They were quite prepared to name well-known saints such as Peter, Patrick, Brigid and Ita. They were surprised to learn that the process for canonising saints in the Catholic Church did not always exist, and all were fascinated by the prospect of some new saints being added to the long list.

However, hearing that St Paul wrote to the ordinary people in Corinth and called them 'saints' was hard to digest. They knew these ordinary folk were often at war with one another. Could they rightly be called 'saints', and, if so, for what reason? The answer is that everybody baptised in water and the Holy Spirit is a member of the Body of Christ, a stone in the Temple of the Holy Spirit and a child of God the Father. Though sin is a real possibility, one's underlying dignity as 'saint' remains.

> And may the Lord make you increase and abound in love for one another and for all, just as we abound in love for you. And may he so strengthen your hearts in holiness that you may be blameless before our God and Father at the coming of our Lord Jesus with all his saints. (1 Thessalonians 3:12-13)

> The Assumption of the Blessed Virgin is a singular participation in her Son's resurrection and an anticipation of the resurrection of other Christians. (CCC 966)

Arriving at the church, on the feast of the Assumption, I was told that a man had just collapsed and that the ambulance was expected soon. I went to attend him as he lay stretched out on the seat. His wife was beside him and very upset. It looked as if he had just had a massive heart attack; he gasped for breath a few times, but did not respond to questions, and his ears were already very blue. Before the men carried him off on a stretcher to hospital, I had a moment to give him conditional absolution.

Though Jesus asks us always to be ready – for death can strike without any warning – he also offers us hope: in death, we meet our Saviour, the risen Lord. The Gospel of today's feast confirms this offer. Mary, the ever-sinless one, has been taken body and soul into Heaven where she enjoys the fullness of life. This assumption is her sharing in the resurrection of her Son. And since Mary is the first among Christian believers, her assumption is a sign of hope for all the rest of us, who also put our faith in her Son. Where she now is, we all hope to be one day, with the help of God.

> And Mary said, 'My soul magnifies the Lord, and my spirit rejoices in God my Saviour, for he has looked with favour on the lowliness of his servant. Surely, from now on all generations will call me blessed; for the Mighty One has done great things for me, and holy is his name'. (Luke 1:46-49)

> In a wholly singular way she co-operated by her obedience, faith, hope and burning charity in the Saviour's work of restoring supernatural life to souls. For this reason she is a mother to us in the order of grace (Lumen Gentium, 61). (CCC 968)

In the Catholic tradition, Mary the mother of Jesus is celebrated under many different titles. Today we remember her as Our Lady of Sorrow. The moment of her son's crucifixion was for Mary also a crucifying time. She stood, helpless and heartbroken, beneath the cross, watching her son's blood ebb away. She stood in love, in faith and in hope. By so doing, she captures in one movement the entire Christian life.

The life of all of us who follow Jesus Christ begins at baptism when we are plunged into the death and resurrection of Jesus, and our sins are forgiven through the shedding of his blood. This new Christian life is a life of faith in Jesus as God's Son, a life of love for God and neighbour, and a life of hope in the promises of a faithful God. Since Mary first lived this life in its fulness, she is rightly termed the Mother of the Church. Having once given physical birth to Jesus, she now gives spiritual birth to the body of Jesus, which we call the church.

> And that is what the soldiers did. Meanwhile, standing near the cross of Jesus were his mother, and his mother's sister, Mary the wife of Clopas, and Mary Magdalene. When Jesus saw his mother and the disciple whom he loved standing beside her, he said to his mother, 'Woman, here is your son.' Then he said to the disciple, 'Here is your mother.' And from that hour the disciple took her into his own home. (John 19:25-27)

> Were there no forgiveness of sins in the Church, there would be no hope of life to come or eternal liberation. Let us thank God who has given his Church such a gift (St Augustine). (CCC 983)

Some people always seem to see the bright side of life, while others look at the same life but always seem to see the dark side. If you are an optimist, the joy of Easter will thrill you every day. You will need to hear that the risen Jesus, who is alive today, is the same Jesus who suffered and was killed. There is no resurrection without death. For optimists, these readings say: 'Don't hog the sunshine. Admit the dark is also real. Sin lurks there'.

If you are a pessimist, then Easter, resurrection, joy and hope will not be the first thoughts in your mind. As you ponder the horrors of crucifixion, you may feel that Jesus' life ends ignominiously in death. But does it? Faith assures us that death leads to new life. There is no dark night that God leaves ever black. God always makes dawn to follow night, and forgiveness to overpower sin. For pessimists these readings say: 'Death is not everything. Neither is sin. For God is bigger than death and bigger even than sin'.

> Then Peter came and said to him, 'Lord, if another member of the church sins against me, how often should I forgive? As many as seven times?' Jesus said to him, 'Not seven times, but, I tell you, seventy-seven times'. (Matthew 18:21-22)

> Hope in the bodily resurrection of the dead established
> itself as a consequence intrinsic to faith in God as
> creator of the whole man, soul and body. (CCC 992)

On September 10, 2003, my father died in Tallaght
Hospital, after living a long and passionate life. The days
following his death were very strange indeed. So much to
do, so much to think about, so many people offering a
hand of support that one barely has a moment to grieve.
And grieve we all must, for we lost not just a father but a
dear friend as well. In a way, it's almost a double
bereavement.

The Lord gives and the Lord takes away. Dad was a
remarkable gift to everybody he knew; for this we thank
the God of all blessings. He has now been taken
suddenly from us and we feel the pain and loss, but we
also try to imitate his hopeful faith as we offer him back
to God. We pray that God will welcome him to his true
home, and we look forward to meeting Dad once again
at the heavenly banquet, hosted by our Father.

> And as for the dead being raised, have you not
> read in the book of Moses, in the story about the
> bush, how God said to him, 'I am the God of
> Abraham, the God of Isaac, and the God of
> Jacob'? He is God not of the dead, but of the
> living; you are quite wrong. (Mark 12:26-27)

> Because of Christ, Christian death has a positive meaning: 'For me to live is Christ, and to die is gain' (St Paul to the Philippians, 1:21). (CCC 1010)

In 2003, Jim and Tess were sixty years married. To use a Dublin idiom, 'They had a good innings together'. But Jim's health began to get worse on Good Friday, and it was not clear how long he had to live. His last few days were a time of great pain, and all his family, though grieved at his death, were glad he had to suffer no longer. Looking at his peaceful face in the coffin, someone said, 'He's at rest now. You can see it in his features'.

Irish people are very good at attending funerals. They come to the church for the removal, and many attend the funeral Mass the next day and follow the hearse to the cemetery. Death is a normal part of life; everybody feels the death of close family and friends and relishes the support of the community when they are bereaved. Every funeral we attend is a rehearsal for our own. With our faith to assist us, we try to let go of life and give it back to the God who first bestowed it.

> The saying is sure: If we have died with him, we will also live with him. (2 Timothy 2:11)

The Church encourages us to prepare ourselves for the hour of our death. (CCC 1014)

Some day will be our last day on earth. Some day each one of us will die and come face to face with Our Lord and Master, Jesus Christ. We are absolutely certain this meeting will take place, but nobody knows for sure when or how. That's why he advises us to always be on the alert, always ready. He wants us to be like boy scouts, always watching out and always living our life so that we are well prepared to meet him when he comes.

Jesus does not want us to be afraid of his coming. He comes with salvation to heal our brokenness, so there's no need for fearful or hysterical waiting. The best way to wait is to continue doing our work as best we can day by day so that, in fact, every day becomes a day fit to meet him. The best time to prepare for death is not when death comes knocking on our doorstep – the best time is now. We should try to live every day as if it were our last. One day we'll get it absolutely right.

But we do not want you to be uninformed, brothers and sisters, about those who have died, so that you may not grieve as others do who have no hope. For since we believe that Jesus died and rose again, even so, through Jesus, God will bring with him those who have died. (1 Thessalonians 4:13-14)

> Heaven is the ultimate end and fulfilment of the deepest human longings, the state of supreme, definitive happiness. (CCC 1024)

In Dunquin, the most westward parish in Kerry, there is a beautiful interpretive centre celebrating the people of the Blasket Islands and their fascinating culture. While lamenting, along with Tomás Ó Criomhthain, that 'their likes will never be found again', the visitor can also rejoice in so much living literature emerging from such a tiny centre. Wild the place may have been, but wise were its folk, beyond our expectations.

Peig Sayers was unable to read or write in any language, and yet she could recite by heart over three hundred tales from Gaelic Ireland. Through her memory came the wisdom of an ancient people. 'There are no more valuable jewels', she said, 'than these two: youth and health'. If Heaven means anything, it must be imagined in these terms. Eternal youth and perpetual health are what we long for: God renews our youth and God heals our brokenness.

> But, as it is written, 'What no eye has seen, nor ear heard, nor the human heart conceived, what God has prepared for those who love him' – these things God has revealed to us through the Spirit; for the Spirit searches everything, even the depths of God. (1 Corinthians 2:9-10)

All who die in God's grace and friendship, but still imperfectly purified, are indeed assured of their eternal salvation: but after death they undergo purification, so as to achieve the holiness necessary to enter the joy of heaven. (CCC 1030)

On the feast of All Souls we pray for our brothers and sisters who have died and are now in Purgatory. This is a very old tradition, with roots in our Jewish heritage and with a long development throughout our Catholic history. What can we say about this strange mystery of our faith? Is Purgatory a real place, or might it be better, perhaps, to talk about a state of being rather than a place? Is the process of purification a helpful image for making sense of Purgatory?

Or might it be helpful to imagine life's journey back to God after the manner of a long-distance race, for which some have trained harder than others and some, being less fit, are still in need of more training? Or, again, might we not think about God the potter who shapes us after the image of his Son, but, finding the image somewhat blurred in some of us, needs to redo the moulding and the firing so that a better image may be produced?

In doing this he acted very well and honourably, taking account of the resurrection. For if he were not expecting that those who had fallen would rise again, it would have been superfluous and foolish to pray for the dead. But if he was looking to the splendid reward that is laid up for those who fall asleep in godliness, it was a holy and pious thought. Therefore he made atonement for the dead, so that they might be delivered from their sin. (2 Maccabees 12:43-45)

> Our Lord warns us that we shall be separated from him if we fail to meet the serious needs of the poor and the little ones who are his brethren … This state of definitive self-exclusion from communion with God and the blessed is called 'hell'. (CCC 1033)

People making complaints to Threshold, the national housing organisation, have described abominable living conditions in some privately rented properties. Some people have to live in rooms without windows. Imagine being without the natural light of day, and the effect this would have on the spirit of anyone unfortunate enough to have to exist there. This could hardly be called living – how could a landlord offer such a 'facility' for rent?

Now consider Ailesbury Road, Dublin 4: a delightful picture of a spacious family home, bright and attractive, with extensive windows to allow the full range of God's bright colours in. The auctioneer has quoted €5.85 million for this two-storey, five-bedroom house. One wishes the family well as they dispose of a valued asset. But one wonders how such wealth and beauty can co-exist with such poverty and ugliness in one of the richest countries on earth.

> We know that we have passed from death to life because we love one another. Whoever does not love abides in death. All who hate a brother or sister are murderers, and you know that murderers do not have eternal life abiding in them. (1 John 3:14-15)

> May your creed be for you as a mirror. Look at yourself in it, to see if you believe everything you say you believe. And rejoice in your faith each day (St Augustine). (CCC 1064)

The third Sunday of Advent is called GAUDETE Sunday – REJOICE Sunday. Is it possible to rejoice when there is so much unmerited suffering, famine and warfare? Two thousand years ago in Jerusalem, the intensely hated Romans were the ruling political power. Young men in revolt were being crucified daily, and their bleached skeletons were dangling in the breeze beside every road in Judaea. There were quislings everywhere, lining their pockets with money taken in taxes for the Roman masters.

Then, out of the desert came forth a strong, resounding voice. It was John the Baptist and he had good news for the people: 'There is a way forward', he said, 'There is a way to reach peace: let him who has two coats share with him who has none'. One of the most heartening things every year is that so many people make such generous responses to the St Vincent de Paul collections all over Ireland.

> For in him every one of God's promises is a 'Yes'. For this reason it is through him that we say the 'Amen,' to the glory of God. (2 Corinthians 1:20)

PART TWO

The Celebration
of the
Christian Mystery

The Paschal Mystery in the Age of the Church

> A better knowledge of the Jewish people's faith and religious life as professed and lived even now can help our better understanding of certain aspects of Christian liturgy. (CCC 1096)

The year 2005 saw the first cohort of Irish students to take Religious Education as part of the Leaving Certificate examination. They received very good results: all seventy-six students took the higher level paper and all passed. Teachers admitted that the course was difficult, but that the questions were fair. Will more students now follow their example and face the challenge of quite a demanding paper?

These are some of the questions posed that year: 'Outline the evidence for the existence of God provided in the writings of either Anselm or Aquinas.' 'Describe the characteristics of the Kingdom of God as preached by Jesus.' '"Stewardship and care of the earth is part of the story of world religions." Discuss this statement with reference to one of the following world religions: Buddhism, Christianity, Hinduism, Islam, Judaism'. How would you fare, do you think?

> Your lamb shall be without blemish, a year-old male. You shall keep it until the fourteenth day of this month; then the whole assembled congregation of Israel shall slaughter it at twilight. (Exodus 12:5-6)

The grace of the Holy Spirit seeks to awaken faith, conversion of heart and adherence to the Father's will. (CCC 1098)

In the lead up to the recent census, the enumerators called to leave in a lengthy form and promised to collect it when it had been completed. All the usual questions about the household are there: how many people, how many rooms, what about central heating, water and sewerage? What is your educational attainment and what kind of work do you do? These are important questions for the government to know.

There were also some new questions. What is your nationality? Do you have a PC? Are you connected to the Internet? These issues reflect a changing Ireland. Change can be a burden, but it can also bring new blessings. When Jesus preached the Kingdom of God and invited people to a radical change of heart (conversion), he was offering the kind of profound change that leads to new life and happiness.

Now after John was arrested, Jesus came to Galilee, proclaiming the good news of God, and saying, 'The time is fulfilled, and the kingdom of God has come near; repent, and believe in the good news'. (Mark 1:14-15)

The Sacramental Celebration of the Paschal Mystery

> Mother Church earnestly desires that all the faithful should be led to that full, conscious and active participation in liturgical celebrations which is demanded by the very nature of the liturgy (Vatican II, on the Liturgy). (CCC 1141)

Rehearsals for a play can be tedious affairs. Words must be learnt by heart; movements have to be practised again and again; co-ordination must be established between all the players on stage. But there is a drama at work below the surface. The poetic language of the playwright brings constant delight, and new insights into words and phrases emerge unexpectedly. Shared reflection on a common text brings added appreciation to all.

Life too can be like that: often boring, yet full of light beams falling on dark corners. Liturgy too can be like life and drama rehearsals: repetitive and numbing at times, uplifting and inspirational at others. One way of lessening the tedium and increasing the power of liturgy is to help people engage in it with a full, active and conscious participation.

> But you are a chosen race, a royal priesthood, a holy nation, God's own people, in order that you may proclaim the mighty acts of him who called you out of darkness into his marvelous light. (1 Peter 2:9)

The harmony of signs (song, music, words and actions) is all the more expressive and fruitful when expressed in the cultural richness of the People of God who celebrate. (CCC 1158)

Cycling on the Navan Road I met the tail end of a huge traffic jam, stretching from Fairyhouse back to Blanchardstown Shopping Centre. At first I thought there might have been an accident, but then I noticed a lot of busses, and many young adults getting off and walking on the hard shoulder. Clearly they were on their way to a rock concert close by. Many probably never got there.

Not everybody enjoys the heavy rhythm of rock bands, but many young people would die for it. They are prepared to pay big money and waste long hours and travel great distances just to be with their friends and have a day out. How can the energy, enthusiasm and aestheticism associated with these great secular liturgies be brought to bear on the central Christian celebrations?

O come, let us sing to the LORD; let us make a joyful noise to the rock of our salvation! Let us come into his presence with thanksgiving; let us make a joyful noise to him with songs of praise! For the LORD is a great God, and a great King above all gods. (Psalms 95:1-3)

> Christian iconography expresses in images the same Gospel message that Scripture communicates by words. (CCC 1160)

I had seen the mosaics on an earlier visit to Sicily and I knew we would be impressed. Entering Monreale Cathedral from the side, we looked up towards the apse and saw the impressive face of Christ the King. Standing in the centre aisle, looking left and right at the story of salvation that is told with such clarity, we admired the skill of the artists. We heard that the Norman rulers employed the Muslim Arabs (though they closed their Mosques) to construct the elegant building for these mosaics.

Then the electric light went out. We could barely see the mosaics. We felt annoyed; we had so little time to see so much beauty. Somebody put a coin in the box and the lights shone again – the day was saved! Later, however, we heard a fine reflection on light: when first built, these mosaics were lit by daylight, with some aid from candles only. Yet people then had time to browse, time to look deeply and time to reflect. Electric light, though a blessing, can also be a curse.

> He is the image of the invisible God, the firstborn of all creation; for in him all things in heaven and on earth were created, things visible and invisible, whether thrones or dominions or rulers or powers – all things have been created through him and for him. (Colossians 1:15-16)

> Sunday is the pre-eminent day for the liturgical assembly, when the faithful gather 'to listen to the word of God ... giving thanks to God'. (CCC 1167)

When we gather for Mass we shout aloud our thanks to God for all he means to us. That part of the Mass is called the Eucharistic, or thanksgiving prayer. Here, in the heart of the Mass, we celebrate God the Father who raised Jesus Christ from the dead and allowed forgiveness for sins to flow like soothing, balmy oil over sinful people. We join Naaman, the Syrian, and the Samaritan leper in saying thanks for healing and forgiveness. But it's not enough merely to join in this prayer.

Seamus Heaney, when he won the Nobel Prize for literature, reminded us that we are a verbal people. Often we believe that, once we have spoken, it is done; but that is not always the case. We still have to match words with action. We still have to 'make thanks' and not just 'say thanks'. One way to do this is to pledge in every Mass that we will bring God's gifts of healing and forgiveness into our work, our friendships and our social life. Then our saying thanks will be true thanksgiving. Our Mass will be more than mere words; it will be the pulse of our life as well.

> When he was at the table with them, he took bread, blessed and broke it, and gave it to them. Then their eyes were opened, and they recognised him; and he vanished from their sight. (Luke 24:30-31)

> The visible church is a symbol of the Father's house towards which the People of God is journeying and where the Father will wipe every tear from their eyes. (CCC 1186)

The church of the Holy Cross in Clonliffe College has ceased regular liturgical services. For about a hundred and fifty years it served the needs of the community of the seminary, and functioned also as a chapel of ease for the locality. On some occasions it witnessed ordinations, or adult confirmations, or graduation masses for the Mater Dei Institute of Education. Musical concerts were also staged there.

The spacious sanctuary area was adapted three years ago for the Mater Dei drama group. Even though the play had a church feel to it (T.S. Eliot's *Murder in the Cathedral)*, there was some raising of eyebrows. However, this was surely unnecessary, for when the Roman Christians were first able to select a style of building for their community liturgies, instead of going for the religious-looking temples, they adapted the secular basilica model. This is the actual pattern of Clonliffe Church. We might also recall that liturgy and drama have much in common: one is communal celebration of God at work, the other is God's creatures at work in play.

> And I heard a loud voice from the throne saying, 'See, the home of God is among mortals. He will dwell with them; they will be his peoples, and God himself will be with them; he will wipe every tear from their eyes. Death will be no more; mourning and crying and pain will be no more, for the first things have passed away'. (Revelation 21:3-4)

> The celebration of the liturgy, therefore, should correspond to the genius and culture of the different peoples. (CCC 1204)

Mellieha Bay, in the north-west of Malta, is where we once went on holidays. After our first meal, we explored the sea-front. There was a smell of barbecues and food cooking. We saw a most amazing sight: between the footpath and the water there was a narrow walkway about fifteen feet wide. Seated around simple tables, heaped with cups, bottles, bread and other foodstuffs were hundreds of locals.

While fathers prepared food, some children were still in the shallow water (it was almost dark by now) and mothers tended the very young. Every nation has its own unique customs. Perhaps this seafront barbecue is a Maltese one. As an island people, they are clearly very much at ease with the sea. Not far from this very spot, St Paul was shipwrecked nearly two thousand years ago.

> Now to God who is able to strengthen you according to my gospel and the proclamation of Jesus Christ, according to the revelation of the mystery that was kept secret for long ages but is now disclosed, and through the prophetic writings is made known to all the Gentiles, according to the command of the eternal God, to bring about the obedience of faith – to the only wise God, through Jesus Christ, to whom be the glory forever! Amen. (Romans 16:25-27)

The Sacraments of Christian Initiation

> Holy Baptism is the basis of the whole Christian life, the gateway to life in the Spirit, and the door which gives access to the other sacraments. (CCC 1213)

Our cluster of ten parishes in Dublin's north inner city has been working together for a few years on a common project: to revitalise our existing baptism teams and to help the emergence of new ones. There is some dissatisfaction about the practice of celebrating infant baptism. What people are looking for in baptism is often not clear: the work of preparing the parents and godparents for the big day is sometimes well done, but sometimes not so; the baptism teams encounter many new problems; and the actual liturgy of baptism needs to be evaluated.

Baptism is the foundational sacrament in the Christian life. From it derives our dignity as children of God, our identity as members of the Body of Christ and our destiny as temples of the Holy Spirit. Given its clear importance, why is it often undervalued or simply misunderstood? Why is so little social importance attached to baptism, by contrast to the days of First Communion and Confirmation?

> Do you not know that all of us who have been baptised into Christ Jesus were baptised into his death? Therefore we have been buried with him by baptism into death, so that, just as Christ was raised from the dead by the glory of the Father, so we too might walk in newness of life. (Romans 6:3-4)

The Second Vatican Council restored for the Latin Church 'the catechumenate for adults, comprising several distinct steps'. The rites for these stages are to be found in the Rite of Christian Initiation of Adults (RCIA). (CCC 1232)

On the feast of St Agatha, we celebrated not only our patron saint but also the riches of our local faith community. At evening Mass, there was a long procession of people representing a variety of ministries in the parish. We rejoiced in readers and ministers of the Eucharist, in cleaners and money collectors, in singers and in prayer groups. The Christian Brothers and Daughters of Charity were there. There were those who care for the elderly and offer bereavement counselling, and those who offer a welcome hand at the door.

Everybody brought forward a symbol of their involvement within the life of the parish. The person who caught the eye of many had a delightful smile, and was carrying up a big bowl of water: Kirsty is from Sweden and she is engaged to be married to the son of a parishioner. Together with a few other adults, she is now preparing for baptism at Easter. *The Rite of Christian Initiation of Adults* is beginning to make an impact in the North Inner City.

You have been born anew, not of perishable but of imperishable seed, through the living and enduring word of God. (1 Peter 1:23)

> Baptism is performed in the most expressive way by triple immersion in the baptismal water. (CCC 1240)

When infants are baptised with the pouring of a few drops of water, something very important is missing. Though a profound spiritual transformation takes place, those who are gathered around the font must take it entirely on faith. The usual minimal gestures are slow to reveal the hidden work of God on the human soul. A different dynamic occurs when baptism involves immersion in water. The same inner change takes place, but the people assembled now have a wonderful aid to faith: the power of the ritual and the vitality of the symbolic action touch their imagination in an unforgettable way.

Some new churches in Ireland have developed pools for baptism. While this is not a real option in most parishes in the immediate future, perhaps some rethinking of the ritual of baptism is necessary. Could the font be placed in a more striking position, given that baptism is the fundamental Christian sacrament? Could water be poured with greater abandon? Could chrism be more liberally poured over the head? Could the celebration of baptism be incorporated more often in the worship of the entire parish?

> Jesus answered him, 'Very truly, I tell you, no one can see the kingdom of God without being born from above.' Nicodemus said to him, 'How can anyone be born after having grown old? Can one enter a second time into the mother's womb and be born?' Jesus answered, 'Very truly, I tell you, no one can enter the kingdom of God without being born of water and Spirit'. (John 3:3-5)

> The white garment symbolises that the person baptised has 'put on Christ', has risen with Christ. (CCC 1243)

The eighth Sunday after Easter is the day of the Holy Spirit, Pentecost or Whit Sunday; this is the day we celebrate the birth of the Church. 'Spirit Day' reminds us that God's greatest gift to the world flows from the death and resurrection of Jesus. That gift is God's Spirit, or God's very life, poured out into the hearts of all those who believe in Jesus. The word 'Pentecost' reminds us also of the Jewish feast of first fruits, fifty days after Passover. The Holy Spirit is truly the first fruits of Jesus' death and resurrection.

We call this day 'Whit Sunday' in memory of the white clothes worn by the newly baptised people during the fifty days of the Easter Season. Baptised into Christ at the Easter vigil, they then began to wear their new white clothes, a sign of their new dignity as children of God. All together, believing in the Father and in the Son and in the Holy Spirit, they constitute the Church of Jesus Christ.

> As many of you as were baptised into Christ have clothed yourselves with Christ. There is no longer Jew or Greek, there is no longer slave or free, there is no longer male and female; for all of you are one in Christ Jesus. (Galatians 3:27-28)

> The practice of infant baptism is an immemorial tradition of the Church. There is explicit testimony to this practice from the second century on, and it is quite possible that, from the beginning of the apostolic preaching, when whole 'households' received Baptism, infants may also have been baptised. (CCC 1252)

It was an unusual Christening; Isobel is neither an infant nor an adult. She is a young child, well able to speak up for herself, but still requiring the support of her parents. Though I directed most of the questions towards her parents and godparents, I still felt obliged to ask her a few. On one occasion, when I asked her if she was happy to go on with the ceremony, she said she wasn't sure. But the eyes of her mother suggested otherwise.

The practical issue that most concerned her mother was the Christening robe. There was no point in imagining her daughter to be a child but, since she is clearly not an adult yet, there was no attempt to dress her in the long white robe. A compromise was reached. Her aunt brought her a neat white top that tied below her neck. It was by no means high fashion, but it was enough to echo the phrase of St Paul about 'putting on Christ', something that happens in every baptism.

> A certain woman named Lydia, a worshiper of God, was listening to us; she was from the city of Thyatira and a dealer in purple cloth. The Lord opened her heart to listen eagerly to what was said by Paul. When she and her household were baptised, she urged us, saying, 'If you have judged me to be faithful to the Lord, come and stay at my home.' And she prevailed upon us. (Acts 16:14-15)

> Baptism makes us members of the Body of Christ ...
> By Baptism they share in the priesthood of Christ, in
> his prophetic and royal mission. (CCC 1267-1268)

The Good Shepherd theme of today's Gospel invites deep reflection. God has appointed Jesus to care for us, the way God used to care for his Chosen people. The Good Shepherd has his work cut out in a world full of thieves and brigands, who seduce people into death. Rather than following such bad leads, the faithful need to go with their Good Shepherd, who guarantees them a safe haven.

However, today is not just about sheep who follow. This Gospel also suggests an active, caring role for all who belong to Christ, for all who are part of his body. As people baptised into Christ, all the followers or disciples are truly part of the mystery of Christ at work in the world. They are his eyes, his hands, his heart, his outreach. Like him, they have a vocation to be good shepherds, caring for all in need.

> For just as the body is one and has many members,
> and all the members of the body, though many, are
> one body, so it is with Christ. For in the one Spirit
> we were all baptised into one body – Jews or
> Greeks, slaves or free – and we were all made to
> drink of one Spirit. (1 Corinthians 12:12-13)

> Baptism constitutes the foundation of communion among all Christians, including those who are not yet in full communion with the Catholic Church. (CCC 1271)

On the very day the new Pope was initiating his pastoral ministry in Rome, we were preparing for the children's Sunday Mass, and they were practising the readings assigned to them. When Antioch was mentioned, I told them it was the city where Jesus' followers were first called 'Christians'. The nickname stuck, and here we are, 'Christians' today. One of the young girls said, 'I thought we were Catholics'.

As I went on to talk about Catholic Christians, I was thinking of the beautiful homily of Pope Benedict earlier that day, and especially his reaching out to our separated brethren. This is what he said: 'With great affection I also greet all those who have been reborn in the sacrament of Baptism but are not yet in full communion with us'. My hope and prayer is that these words will give birth to new ecumenical initiatives, based on our common baptism into Jesus Christ.

> Then Barnabas went to Tarsus to look for Saul, and when he had found him, he brought him to Antioch. So it was that for an entire year they met with the church and taught a great many people, and it was in Antioch that the disciples were first called 'Christians'. (Acts 11:25-26)

> Give them the spirit of wisdom and understanding, the spirit of right judgement and courage, the spirit of knowledge and reverence. (CCC 1299)

In the distance he seemed quite odd, because he was wearing a helmet which didn't fit well. As he stopped at the lights and I cycled up behind him, I noticed a small bag on his back carrier. It was rice and the address of the producer was Thailand. I remembered a letter sent home recently by my nephew, who told us he was drinking a pint in a bar and reading the *Bangkok Times* to get the results of football matches, when he saw an article about Ballyferriter and the West Kerry Gaeltacht.

More and more one gets the sense of the world becoming a much smaller place. People can turn up anywhere. Often the stranger is unwelcome, because fearful humans wonder how the newcomers might threaten them. We need to recall 'courage', one of the gifts of the Holy Spirit poured out on us in Confirmation. Jesus regularly had to advise his followers: 'Fear not!'

> I have said this to you, so that in me you may have peace. In the world you face persecution. But take courage; I have conquered the world! (John 16:33)

> [C]atechesis for Confirmation should strive to awaken a sense of belonging to the Church of Jesus Christ, the universal Church as well as the parish community. (CCC 1309)

It was a very special meeting to discuss problems connected with Confirmation in the North Inner City. All the major actors were there: parents, school principals, schoolteachers, school chaplains, members of boards of management and parish clergy. In small groups composed of like people everybody answered a simple question, 'As somebody involved in preparing children for Confirmation, what are your major concerns?'

The concerns of one group might not match those of another. But some common issues did emerge. Are the children too young? Is Confirmation a sacrament of faith or just a big day out? What is supposed to happen in Confirmation? There was unanimous agreement about the quality of work being done in school by the teachers. There was less satisfaction about the contribution of parents and priests. Finding some ways to rectify this situation will not be easy.

> Now when the apostles at Jerusalem heard that Samaria had accepted the word of God, they sent Peter and John to them. The two went down and prayed for them that they might receive the Holy Spirit (for as yet the Spirit had not come upon any of them; they had only been baptised in the name of the Lord Jesus). Then Peter and John laid their hands on them, and they received the Holy Spirit. (Acts 8:14-17)

> The miracles of the multiplication of the loaves, when the Lord says the blessing, breaks and distributes the loaves through his disciples to feed the multitude, prefigure the superabundance of this unique bread of his Eucharist. (CCC 1335)

There is something very impressive about the Gospel story of Jesus and his disciples feeding thousands of hungry folk at the lakeshore. The author of the Gospel gives an account of this feeding in the exact same words as he uses for describing the Last Supper. On both occasions, by the lake and at the supper, Jesus took bread, said the regular blessing prayer, broke the bread and gave it to the people.

The taking, blessing, breaking and giving which marked both feeding stories in the Gospel are the very same activities at the heart of each Mass offered today. Every Mass involves the priest (in the person of Christ) taking bread and wine from the assembled people, saying the blessing prayer over these gifts, then breaking the bread and distributing Holy Communion to all who come forward in faith.

> Then he ordered the crowds to sit down on the grass. Taking the five loaves and the two fish, he looked up to heaven, and blessed and broke the loaves, and gave them to the disciples, and the disciples gave them to the crowds. And all ate and were filled; and they took up what was left over of the broken pieces, twelve baskets full. And those who ate were about five thousand men, besides women and children. (Matthew 14:19-21)

> The Eucharist and the Cross are stumbling blocks.
> It is the same mystery and it never ceases to be an
> occasion of division. (CCC 1336)

The feast of Corpus Christi has moved from Thursday to
Sunday. Gone are the days of solemn processions
following the sacred host through the streets of Dublin.
Traffic makes this next to impossible. The loss is
obvious: people in the streets no longer come face to face
with the paradox of Christian faith. They no longer
confront in public the scandalous mystery at the heart of
Christianity.

Corpus Christi developed as a public feast in the Middle
Ages in Europe. People then still largely believed in the
Christian message. They knew that God was on their
side, in spite of their sin. They knew that Jesus, dead and
risen, was still available to them in their sin, so that by
taking and eating him they could have eternal life. Have
we lost something of this Eucharistic faith? Do we truly
believe that, in taking and eating, we are taking and
eating the risen Lord?

> 'This is the bread that came down from heaven,
> not like that which your ancestors ate, and they
> died. But the one who eats this bread will live
> forever.' He said these things while he was teaching
> in the synagogue at Capernaum. When many of his
> disciples heard it, they said, 'This teaching is
> difficult; who can accept it?' (John 6:58-60)

The liturgy of the Word includes 'the writings of the prophets' ... and 'the memoirs of the apostles' (their letters and the Gospels). After the homily, which is an exhortation to accept this Word as what it truly is, the Word of God, and to put it into practice, come the intercessions for all men. (CCC 1349)

Studying the *Catechism of Trent*, which offered parish priests material to help them prepare their sermons, one student inquired if priests were obliged to preach today at Sunday Mass. He said his own parish priest (the only priest in the parish) gives homilies only at Christmas and Easter. He assumed that this was quite normal and, when told it was the reverse, wondered if he should report his priest. How else can the parishioners hear the word of God?

His last comment makes much sense. The people of God are built up on the foundation of God's word, made flesh in Jesus, and proclaimed in every Eucharist. If their pastors fail to provide them with this foundation, perhaps their life of faith will collapse. This consideration led on to another reflection: given that so many people today no longer come to Sunday Mass, how are they meant to hear the Good News of Jesus Christ? These are challenging times indeed.

We also constantly give thanks to God for this, that when you received the word of God that you heard from us, you accepted it not as a human word but as what it really is, God's word, which is also at work in you believers. (1 Thessalonians 2:13)

> The Eucharist is a sacrifice of thanksgiving to the Father, a blessing by which the Church expresses her gratitude to God for all his benefits, for all that he has accomplished through creation, redemption and sanctification. Eucharist means first of all 'thanksgiving'. (CCC 1360)

The Catholic Church in Dublin has much to repent of, but also much to be proud of. Our new Coadjutor Archbishop, Diarmuid Martin, promised that the Church would never forget the hurt of those who have lost the faith because clerics abused them sexually. He also spoke movingly about those people who remain faithful, in spite of the shock of this abuse. Then he went on to salute the great wealth of talent and faith among the ordinary Dublin priests.

The TV news concentrated on clerical sexual abuse (CSA) and this is understandable. But the question must be asked, why were none of his positive comments given much prominence? Repentance is only one part of the Mass. Why did the news not also talk about the prayer of thanksgiving, which is even more central? Why was no mention made of the riveting rhythms of the liturgy and their beautiful evocation of the heart of Ireland and the soul of Africa?

> Thanks be to God for his indescribable gift! (2 Corinthians 9:15)

> The Eucharist is the memorial of Christ's Passover, the making present and the sacramental offering of his unique sacrifice, in the liturgy of the Church which is his Body. (CCC 1362)

Sacrifice is a key religious activity. From time immemorial people have sacrificed animals and crops to placate the gods. Jews sacrificed bulls and goats in their Temple, to ask forgiveness and give thanks to Yahweh God. At the heart of Catholic practice is the sacrifice of the Mass. This is a very unusual sacrifice: here the priest, the altar and the offering are all one and the same.

Jesus Christ offers himself to his Father on the cross and, when his followers do this in memory of him, this one sacrifice is made present over and over again. No blood is visible, but real sacrificial offering continues to be made. The value of this offering comes from the love that fills it and the mercy that inspires it. Sacrifice, running over with loving mercy, is the heart of the Christian religion.

> Consequently he is able for all time to save those who approach God through him, since he always lives to make intercession for them. For it was fitting that we should have such a high priest, holy, blameless, undefiled, separated from sinners, and exalted above the heavens. Unlike the other high priests, he has no need to offer sacrifices day after day, first for his own sins, and then for those of the people; this he did once for all when he offered himself. (Hebrews 7:25-27)

> In his Eucharistic presence he remains mysteriously
> in our midst as the one who loved us and gave
> himself up for us. (CCC 1380)

Some time ago we went to *Communion*, a play by Aidan
Mathews in the Peacock. The scene displays a sick bed in
a Dublin suburb. The older brother, Jordan, is dying of a
brain tumour. The younger brother, Marcus, is a manic-
depressive. His girlfriend (a Protestant), the neighbour (a
Methodist), the priest (a family friend) just home from
Rwanda, and the boys' mother make up the rest of the
cast. Mass begins with reflection on the human
condition; the readings and prayers follow.

Just when we expect the Liturgy of the Eucharist to begin, the
play comes to an abrupt halt. Jordan screams from the
depths of his pain and act one finishes. While reflecting on
the scream and observing the light on Jordan's face, I thought
of Jesus at the river Jordan (his place of baptism) and Jesus
on the cross ('My God, my God, why have you forsaken
me?'). Here, in this tortured face, we had the reality of Jesus'
self-sacrifice, which the ritual of the Eucharist makes present
for us today.

> For through the law I died to the law, so that I
> might live to God. I have been crucified with
> Christ; and it is no longer I who live, but it is Christ
> who lives in me. And the life I now live in the flesh I
> live by faith in the Son of God, who loved me and
> gave himself for me. (Galatians 2:19-20)

> The Mass is at the same time, and inseparably, the sacrificial memorial in which the sacrifice of the cross is perpetuated and the sacred banquet of communion with the Lord's body and blood. (CCC 1382)

What can one say about Mel Gibson's film, *The Passion of the Christ*? Is it over-the-top? Is it suitable for children? Might it spark off a new phase of anti-semitism? Having watched it recently, my first assessment is fundamentally positive. While there are items I didn't like (a too literal reading of the Temple veil being torn in two), and a few scenes I couldn't understand (no obvious Biblical echo), the film overall was a powerful telling of the story of the Passion.

In particular, I liked the use of flashbacks to make strong theological points. The crucifixion scene, with a mangled and blood-stained Jesus writhing in agony, is interlaced with moments of peace from the Last Supper, the previous evening. What Jesus gave up on Calvary – his body and blood in sacrifice – he had already given to his disciples as bread and wine in the Passover Meal, and asked them to do this in his memory until Kingdom come. Meal, Cross, Mass: the one Jesus.

> So Jesus said to them, 'Very truly, I tell you, unless you eat the flesh of the Son of Man and drink his blood, you have no life in you. Those who eat my flesh and drink my blood have eternal life, and I will raise them up on the last day; for my flesh is true food and my blood is true drink'. (John 6:53-55)

> What material food produces in our bodily life, Holy
> Communion wonderfully achieves in our spiritual
> life. Communion with the flesh of the risen Christ, a
> flesh 'given life and giving life through the Holy
> Spirit', preserves, increases and renews the life of
> grace received at Baptism. (CCC 1392)

After we have sinned, we hunger for forgiveness and
acceptance. This is how God meets that hunger: 'Come to
the Lord's table, all you sinners who have been forgiven'.
Every one of us hungers for recognition. When we
approach the Lord in Holy Communion we are offered the
host one by one, on the hand or on the tongue: 'This is my
body broken for you'. Jesus feeds us and affirms us as
special individuals every time we come to him in faith,
hope and love.

The feast of Corpus Christi, the Body and Blood of Christ,
is a truly remarkable one. For those who believe that the
dead and risen Lord is given to us as food for our life
journey, there can be no despair but only profound hope.
In giving us his beloved Son to take and eat, God our
Father is responding, as only God can, to our deepest
human hungers and our deepest human thirst.

> Those who eat my flesh and drink my blood abide in
> me, and I in them. Just as the living Father sent me,
> and I live because of the Father, so whoever eats me
> will live because of me. This is the bread that came
> down from heaven, not like that which your
> ancestors ate, and they died. But the one who eats
> this bread will live forever. (John 6:56-58)

> To receive in truth the Body and Blood of Christ given up for us, we must recognise Christ in the poorest, his brethren. (CCC 1397)

Julian Filochowski had worked for CAFOD, the English Bishops' agency for poor people overseas, for years. He spoke passionately to us about the extent of poverty in the world today. The irony of his remarks was very obvious – we were seated in a hotel room in Los Angeles, California, the wealthiest state on earth. He told us, among other things, that in 2003 over 1.2 billion people existed on $1 per day or less.

The most interesting part of his talk was when he read from a letter written by St John Chrysostom sixteen centuries ago to his people in Constantinople, where he was Bishop. The problems then were very similar: some very wealthy people lived in a world of extreme poverty. Christian stewardship of the earth implies that everybody deserves to have what is needed for life. Those who have too much ought to share generously with those who have too little.

> Then the righteous will answer him, 'Lord, when was it that we saw you hungry and gave you food, or thirsty and gave you something to drink? And when was it that we saw you a stranger and welcomed you, or naked and gave you clothing? And when was it that we saw you sick or in prison and visited you?' And the king will answer them, 'Truly I tell you, just as you did it to one of the least of these who are members of my family, you did it to me'. (Matthew 25:37-40)

> The Church warmly recommends that the faithful receive Holy Communion each time they participate in the celebration of the Eucharist; she obliges them to do so at least once a year. (CCC 1417)

'I am the bread of life'. This is how Jesus describes himself today. Looking into the past, he reminds the crowd of the faithfulness of God, who always fed his chosen people during their time in the desert. But this new 'bread of life' is going to be something very special. It will be the very Son of God himself, given to us as food to eat, and offered to us to satisfy all our hungers. 'All who take and eat will never go hungry'.

During the Last Supper, when Jesus first 'took, blessed, broke and gave' himself as bread to his disciples to eat, he also did something very strange – he took a basin of water and washed the feet of his disciples. This was his way of teaching a very special message about 'the bread of life'. One of its main purposes is to fit people for service. All those who have been fed ought to kneel down in service of one another.

> Jesus said to them, 'I am the bread of life. Whoever comes to me will never be hungry, and whoever believes in me will never be thirsty'. (John 6:35)

> Because Christ himself is present in the sacrament of the altar, he is to be honoured with the worship of adoration. (CCC 1418)

Our final year undergraduates are too young to remember the Catholic Church we grew up in. Born since 1980, they remember only a vernacular liturgy with congregational singing, ministers of the word, Eucharist in the hand and active participation. The Latin Mass is a foreign concept; Benediction almost unknown. One of our students recalled being at Benediction in India, where the practice still flourishes. He wondered, why has it disappeared in Ireland?

We searched for some reasons. It can't be due to Roman policy; Benediction is still encouraged, as a way of meditating on the real presence of Christ in the Blessed Eucharist. The more likely reason for the neglect of this practice is the pragmatic one of Sunday Evening Mass and the consequent problem of timing. A further cultural factor could well be the colonisation of Sunday as a day of rest and prayer. Will Benediction make a recovery?

> Therefore, since we are receiving a kingdom that cannot be shaken, let us give thanks, by which we offer to God an acceptable worship with reverence and awe; for indeed our God is a consuming fire. (Hebrews 12:28-29)

The Sacraments of Healing

> The Lord Jesus Christ, physician of our souls and bodies, who forgave the sins of the paralytic and restored him to bodily health, has willed that his Church continue, in the power of the Holy Spirit, his work of healing and salvation, even among her own members. (CCC 1421)

I can see the ceiling of the Sistine Chapel in Rome with Michelangelo's painting of the creation. The beardless man reclining with one hand raised; the bearded one above him stretching forth a creative hand. Both hands almost touch – a life touch. I see midwife hands supporting the head, cutting the cord and patting the back until a cry proves that life is renewed. I see other hands too. These are grasping and gripping, describing a circle of lust – a vicious circle called rape. I can see tender hands entwined in the liturgy of love.

I can also see hands that are writing. Fingers holding pens dipped into poison. Others drawing hearts on a Valentine card. Some hands I see have forefingers pressing submachine gun triggers. Others are guiding a scalpel through a cancerous growth. I can see a young man stretch out a hand of pity and touch the untouchable – and the leper is cleansed. What hands have we?

> 'Which is easier, to say to the paralytic, "Your sins are forgiven," or to say, "Stand up and take your mat and walk"? But so that you may know that the Son of Man has authority on earth to forgive sins' – he said to the paralytic – 'I say to you, stand up, take your mat and go to your home.' And he stood up, and immediately took the mat and went out before all of them; so that they were all amazed and glorified God, saying, 'We have never seen anything like this!' (Mark 2:9-12)

It is called the sacrament of Reconciliation, because it imparts to the sinner the love of God who reconciles. (CCC 1424)

Every year during Lent, we have a Communal Celebration of the Sacrament of Reconciliation. About a hundred people usually attend. We listen to the words of scripture telling us of human sins and of God's mercy. We spend some time reflecting on the inroads that personal sins have made in the lives of each one present. Then everybody goes to a priest (either in public or privately in the confession box) to tell one's own sins, and to receive God's forgiveness.

It's very different from years ago when queues of penitents gathered each Saturday evening outside every box in the church. Sin was a very private affair then. We now recognise not only our personal wrongdoings, but also admit our communal share of sin and guilt. The ceremony tries to reveal to us both the private and the social dimensions of sin and forgiveness. We focus on sin, but far more on God.

So we are ambassadors for Christ, since God is making his appeal through us; we entreat you on behalf of Christ, be reconciled to God.
(2 Corinthians 5:20)

> During the first centuries the reconciliation of Christians who had committed particularly grave sins after their Baptism (for example, idolatry, murder or adultery) was tied to a very rigorous discipline, according to which penitents had to do public penance for their sins, often for years, before receiving reconciliation. (CCC 1447)

When people in the Christian community do wrong, how should we react? The Gospel suggests a firm but discreet approach. First, go as an individual to the offender and quietly try to get him to see the wrong he is doing. If this fails, go in the company of a few others to see if this might convince him of his wrongdoing. After that, if he is still unrepentant, report him to the community. Now that the matter has been made public, a new dynamic arises. If he pays no attention to the community, then excommunicate him.

This, however, is by no means the end of the process. The Christian community should do everything possible to re-integrate the person cast out for doing wrong. Ideally, it should go the extra mile on that person's behalf, because the purpose of the exclusion order is not to condemn the wrongdoer to final separation, but rather to challenge him to see the error of his ways and turn around to come back home.

> If another member of the church sins against you, go and point out the fault when the two of you are alone. If the member listens to you, you have regained that one. But if you are not listened to, take one or two others along with you, so that every word may be confirmed by the evidence of two or three witnesses. If the member refuses to listen to them, tell it to the church; and if the offender refuses to listen even to the church, let such a one be to you as a Gentile and a tax collector. (Matthew 18:15-17)

> The forgiven penitent is reconciled with himself in his inmost being, where he regains his innermost truth. He is reconciled with his brethren whom he has in some way offended and wounded. He is reconciled with the Church. He is reconciled with all creation (Pope John Paul II). (CCC 1469)

Six years ago, on April 23, Pope John Paul II spoke to the American Cardinals in Rome. He stressed the evil of clerical sex abuse and called it a crime. He asked that greater care be taken in the future, when training men for the priesthood, to eliminate anybody with paedophilic tendencies. There was talk that the American Church would try to establish national consistency in its manner of dealing with this great social and ecclesial evil.

It is ironic that this meeting took place on the feast day of St George, who battled with the dragon (the devil and all the forces of evil) and killed it. Clearly evil must be resisted, but how? Should zero tolerance (one strike and you're out) apply when priests abuse children? Is this the only valid response to the evil of sex abuse? What about the other Christian duty to help sinners repent and regain their baptismal purity?

> But we had to celebrate and rejoice, because this brother of yours was dead and has come to life; he was lost and has been found. (Luke 15:32)

> To return to communion with God after having lost it through sin is a process born of the grace of God who is rich in mercy and solicitous for the salvation of men. (CCC 1489)

A few years ago, the controversial *Power to Change* ads were screened on ITV and other foreign channels, which were not affected by the Irish Broadcasting Act. The ads also appeared on billboards throughout Ireland. We saw the faces of a one-time drug addict and the father of a child killed in the Troubles. The message was the same: through their faith in Jesus Christ people are transformed. They find a power to change.

When Jesus preached in Israel, his message was very simple: the Kingdom of God is at work in the world, so turn away from sin and be converted. Conversion such as this involves a radical change of heart, of mind and of will. No human can achieve this kind of change simply by wanting to make it. However, each person who truly wants to change has a guarantee from Jesus that inner strength will be given to him. This strength or dynamism is called the Holy Spirit of God.

> But God, who is rich in mercy, out of the great love with which he loved us even when we were dead through our trespasses, made us alive together with Christ – by grace you have been saved – and raised us up with him and seated us with him in the heavenly places in Christ Jesus, so that in the ages to come he might show the immeasurable riches of his grace in kindness toward us in Christ Jesus. (Ephesians 2:4-7)

> The movement of return to God, called conversion and repentance, entails sorrow for and abhorrence of sins committed, and a firm purpose of sinning no more in the future. Conversion touches the past and the future, and is nourished by hope in God's mercy. (CCC 1490)

As Christmas Day comes around and family feuds stay alive, how are we to find the energy to become reconciled? Peter once asked Jesus, 'How often should my brother offend me and I still forgive him? As often as seven times?' Peter was being deliberately extravagant, but Jesus flattened him with the following: 'Not seven times, I tell you, but seventy-seven times '. In the Kingdom of God, we have to think big and act big.

The Guinness ad has portrayed this just so. A serious young man strides deliberately out of his office in Dublin, marches across the bogs of Ireland as far as the towering Cliffs of Moher, gazes for a second over the wide Atlantic, then plunges into the deep and swims to New York. After marching through Manhattan and entering a pub, he pauses to look at his friend and then says, 'Sorry'. If reconciliation merits this effort, we are all in great need of God's Holy Spirit.

> Then Peter came and said to him, 'Lord, if another member of the church sins against me, how often should I forgive? As many as seven times?' Jesus said to him, 'Not seven times, but, I tell you, seventy-seven times'. (Matthew 18:21-22)

> The penitent's acts are repentance, confession or disclosure of sins to the priest, and the intention to make reparation and do works of reparation. (CCC 1491)

One of the joys of supervising teaching practice is to relax at the back of a class that somebody else is teaching and reflect on the matter of the lesson. On occasion, one gets a new insight into an old, familiar topic. One day the lesson dealt with the twelve steps used by Alcoholics Anonymous. I was enthralled by the entire process – the way somebody must want to stop drinking, begin to trust in a higher power and take a whole range of other steps before healing is possible.

I began to make comparisons with the sacrament of penance. One must first recognise sin in one's life, turn to God for forgiveness, admit the specific sin to a fellow human being, recognise the harm done to others by one's sins, make restitution for the wrongdoing and trust that healing will emerge. A good healing process such as this sacramental one is bound to find parallels in other areas of life. To restore broken humanity one must respect the human condition.

> Repent therefore of this wickedness of yours, and pray to the Lord that, if possible, the intent of your heart may be forgiven you. (Acts 8:22)

[The Church] believes in the life-giving presence of Christ, the physician of souls and bodies. (CCC 1509)

One of the major social problems of adolescents, of which we are only now beginning to take account, is self-harm. Teachers, counsellors and chaplains have been dealing with this for years, but they have often struggled either to understand its origins or to provide a valid response. They have regularly been unable to adequately help their pupils, trapped in this 'addiction of the millennium'.

Even as its causes have been discovered, and medical and psychological strategies developed, an underlying spiritual issue still needs to be addressed. A person who goes this far in inflicting pain on him/herself is clearly trying to tell us something: 'There is something broken deep down in this heart; can anyone fix it?' A chaplain, recalling the story of the transfigured Christ, may hope to offer some healing: all human suffering, even the most frightening, can be transformed into life by the power of God.

Are any among you sick? They should call for the elders of the church and have them pray over them, anointing them with oil in the name of the Lord. The prayer of faith will save the sick, and the Lord will raise them up; and anyone who has committed sins will be forgiven. (James 5:14-15)

> The first grace of this sacrament [of the sick] is one of strengthening, peace and courage to overcome the difficulties that go with the condition of serious illness or the frailty of old age. (CCC 1520)

We used to have the annual Mass for our sick parishioners later on in the year, but bad weather made us change the date to May. Ascension Sunday was the chosen day for this year. That tied in very well with the theme of the First Reading: Jesus, our brother, has gone through death to a new life; where he has gone, we hope to follow, for he is not just our brother, we are all members of his body, and the members cannot be separated from the head. Therein lies our hope.

To be sick is often to be alone or depressed. Jesus knew that fact well, which is why he went out of his way to meet sick people and restore them to health. We, the body of Christ today, are called to continue his healing outreach. One way we do this is to gather our sick parishioners and pray over them and anoint them with the holy oils. Though there was a heavy shower this year, and though the Mass was delayed a while, one felt a great sense of peace and healing in the church.

> That evening, at sundown, they brought to him all who were sick or possessed with demons. And the whole city was gathered around the door. And he cured many who were sick with various diseases, and cast out many demons; and he would not permit the demons to speak, because they knew him. (Mark 1:32-34)

The Sacraments at the Service of Communion

> Two other sacraments, Holy Orders and Matrimony, are directed towards the salvation of others ... They confer a particular mission in the Church and serve to build up the People of God. (CCC 1534)

Years ago, I remember him preaching a homily in UCD and telling us the meaning of the name Barnabas. He told us it meant 'Son of Encouragement' and, therefore, could well remind teachers of their major task, namely to encourage their pupils in learning. Recently I had occasion to be present in Terenure Church as Monsignor John Greehy confirmed boys from three local schools. Though John is quite ill, his enthusiasm was remarkable.

You could feel it in his homily, especially when he spoke to the youngsters and challenged them to be courageous. You could sense it equally as John named the many people whom he wished to thank for their involvement; everyone got a special mention and a little personal comment. What moved me and my colleague, Philip, most was when John invited us each to join him in anointing our nephews. The ministry of welcome and encouragement is still alive, thank God.

> So also Christ did not glorify himself in becoming a high priest, but was appointed by the one who said to him, 'You are my Son, today I have begotten you'; as he says also in another place, 'You are a priest forever, according to the order of Melchizedek'. (Hebrews 5:5-6)

> While the common priesthood of the faithful is exercised by the unfolding of baptismal grace – a life of faith, hope and charity, a life according to the Spirit, the ministerial priesthood is at the service of the common priesthood. (CCC 1547)

The retreat master, a Dominican priest, spoke eloquently about one of the great titles given to the Church by the Fathers assembled in Rome for the Second Vatican Council: People of God. He invited us to ponder this simple image, to reflect on its meaning and to begin to consider some of its implications for the life of the Church in Ireland. If this image were ever to become the dominant image, what differences of practice might be possible?

Where the people have centrality, equality is more important than diversity of ministry. Baptism as the sacrament of Church membership regains its priority. The sacrament of Orders is the commissioning of servants within the people, charged with helping the people to become what they are, a holy nation, a priestly people, set apart for the worship of God and the love of mankind.

> So Jesus called them and said to them, 'You know that among the Gentiles those whom they recognise as their rulers lord it over them, and their great ones are tyrants over them. But it is not so among you; but whoever wishes to become great among you must be your servant, and whoever wishes to be first among you must be slave of all. For the Son of Man came not to be served but to serve, and to give his life a ransom for many'. (Mark 10:42-45)

> This priesthood is ministerial. 'That office ... which the Lord committed to the pastors of his people, is in the strict sense of the term a service' (Lumen Gentium, 24). (CCC 1551)

While the Cardinals were in Rome to select a new Pope, we in St Agatha's Parish were debating the kind of person we needed on our Parish Pastoral Council. We identified four requirements: faith, prayer, service and mission. The thought crossed my mind: what applies for councillors might also apply for the Pope.

Is it stretching belief too much to suggest that a good Pope should be a man of deep faith and be able to strengthen us in our discipleship? Are we not right to want our Pope to be a man of prayer, a spiritual leader inviting us to daily prayer. When we look for a servant as our Pope, are we not simply recalling his title, 'servant of the servants of God' and remembering Jesus who washed feet? And is not the task of every believer to be on mission, inviting new disciples to follow the Lord?

> Do not lord it over those in your charge, but be examples to the flock. And when the chief shepherd appears, you will win the crown of glory that never fades away. (1 Peter 5:3-4)

> Episcopal consecration confers, together with the office of sanctifying, also the offices of teaching and ruling. (CCC 1558)

On August 8, 2002, death came quietly to Bishop Jim Kavanagh, retired Auxiliary Bishop of Dublin. He was renowned as a gentleman, who related graciously to everybody he met. As a lecturer, he was always stimulating; as a pastor, he showed great love and concern; as somebody deeply interested in all matters sporting, he was the kind of Irishman whom everybody admired and respected. His love for the Irish language was also a noteworthy facet of his long and active life.

What are bishops for? What kind of person should be ordained a bishop? How should such people be identified? What will God ask dead bishops when they reach the pearly gates? We know what this final question is: how well did you shepherd my people, especially those most in need? Jim Kavanagh had a large and generous heart. I am sure he passed the oral examination without too much trouble.

> Jesus said to them again, 'Peace be with you. As the Father has sent me, so I send you.' When he had said this, he breathed on them and said to them, 'Receive the Holy Spirit. If you forgive the sins of any, they are forgiven them; if you retain the sins of any, they are retained'. (John 20:21-23)

> The function of the bishops' ministry was handed over
> in a subordinate degree to priests so that they might be
> ... co-workers of the Episcopal order for the proper
> fulfilment of the apostolic mission that had been
> entrusted to it by Christ (Presbyterorum ordinis, 2#2).
> (CCC 1562)

When Archbishop Diarmuid Martin formally took office
in the Dublin Diocese, the Council of Priests
automatically lapsed. The Archbishop, knowing that a
new Council would not be elected before September and
not wanting his supply of advice to run dry, invited the
existing Council members to continue to meet over the
summer and make suggestions to him. One set of
recommendations concerned 'the need for priests to own
their Council'.

Though some priests value the Council, others are cynical
about it; others again have little interest in it, and there
are some who do not know what it is meant to be. The
feast of St Thomas today may be of benefit to them all.
Thomas insisted on seeing the risen Lord before he would
believe in Him; many priests need to see for themselves
that the Council truly works. This puts it up to those who
experience its life and worth; they need to find convincing
words to attract the sceptics.

> Every high priest chosen from among mortals is put
> in charge of things pertaining to God on their
> behalf, to offer gifts and sacrifices for sins. He is
> able to deal gently with the ignorant and wayward,
> since he himself is subject to weakness; and because
> of this he must offer sacrifice for his own sins as well
> as for those of the people. And one does not
> presume to take this honour, but takes it only when
> called by God, just as Aaron was. (Hebrews 5:1-4)

> Deacons share in Christ's mission and grace in a special way. The sacrament of Holy Orders marks them with an imprint ('character') which cannot be removed and which configures them to Christ, who made himself the 'deacon' or servant of all. (CCC 1570)

St Laurence, the deacon martyr of the Church of Rome, is commemorated in one of the great Basilicas of the eternal city, San Lorenzo fuori le Mura, which is in the Campo Verano (a great cemetery outside the walls of the ancient city of Rome). As deacon, Laurence was in charge of providing for the material needs of all who had come to the notice of the local Christian community. Along with the Pope of the day, Sixtus II, he was killed in 258 for being a Christian. According to tradition, the manner of his death was very gruesome – he was roasted alive on a gridiron.

The very establishment of deacons is traced in the New Testament to this very practical obligation that falls on the Church, namely to provide people in need with the necessary requirements for civilised living. At the heart of the Church, of course, exists the service of God. But this service demands also a service of the needy, whoever they may be. Because Jesus came to serve and not to be served, service is naturally at the heart of the Church, which is his body on earth today.

> Deacons likewise must be serious, not double-tongued, not indulging in much wine, not greedy for money; they must hold fast to the mystery of the faith with a clear conscience. (1 Timothy 3:8-9)

> The ordained ministers exercise their service for the People of God by teaching, divine worship and pastoral governance. (CCC 1592)

Thirty-five years ago, we were ordained in the chapel of the Irish College in Rome. Our parents and families and friends joined us for the great occasion. Having spent many years in the seminary studying and praying and playing together, we were very keen to continue contact after ordination. We promised to meet every year outside the gates of Clonliffe College, on All-Ireland Hurling Sunday after the big match, and then go for a meal together.

Thankfully, we have kept this promise, and all are still alive and ministering as priests. To quote the Pope when we met him in Rome for our tenth anniversary, 'It's not much, but it is something'. Thirty-five is a bit more, and it's still something to be happy about. Who could have guessed what a variety of lifestyles and challenges we would know during those years! For all of this, for the highs and lows, but above all for the bond of unity that has strengthened during the years, we give heartfelt thanks to God.

> Nevertheless on some points I have written to you rather boldly by way of reminder, because of the grace given me by God to be a minister of Christ Jesus to the Gentiles in the priestly service of the gospel of God, so that the offering of the Gentiles may be acceptable, sanctified by the Holy Spirit. (Romans 15:15-16)

> Although the dignity of this institution [marriage] is not transparent everywhere with the same clarity, some sense of the greatness of the matrimonial union exists in all cultures. (CCC 1603)

Pride and Prejudice, the great English novel by Jane Austen, has been adapted for the stage. It was playing in the Gate Theatre a few years ago, and we enjoyed the superb acting and the witty interpretation of the novel's major themes. The interweaving of Darcy's pride and Elizabeth's prejudice is the heart of the play. But how to find wealthy husbands for five poor young daughters is the main concern of Mrs Bennett, their mother.

The economic dimension of marriage figures more centrally than the romantic. The social value of apt family alliances weighs much more heavily with both parents than does the individual emotional health of their nubile children. The question of weighing values against one another is never far from the surface of the play. Is money all-important? Does romantic love count for much? Do parents know what is truly best for their children's welfare?

> So God created humankind in his image, in the image of God he created them; male and female he created them. God blessed them, and God said to them, 'Be fruitful and multiply, and fill the earth and subdue it; and have dominion over the fish of the sea and over the birds of the air and over every living thing that moves upon the earth'. (Genesis 1:27-28)

> In his preaching Jesus unequivocally taught the original meaning of the union of man and woman as the Creator willed it from the beginning: permission given by Moses to divorce one's wife was a concession to the hardness of hearts. (CCC 1614)

Jesus lived in a Jewish culture that accepted divorce, so he probably knew many divorced people, as well as the varied reasons given by people seeking a divorce. But, according to Jesus, none of these reasons justified divorce. Jesus summed up all of these reasons in the phrase 'hardness of heart', in other words, inability to forgive. As long as this unwillingness to forgive petrified the hearts of married people, there had to be divorce. Jesus recognised this, and also recognised how Moses had once accepted it.

But Jesus saw a deeper reality at work in the world, namely the forgiving love of God. This love was a law even more fundamental than the Law of Moses. When Jesus rejected Moses' law permitting divorce, Jesus appealed to this divine law of forgiving love. This divine love is a love that binds people together, whereas the Law of Moses allowed them to drift apart. That was why the Law of Moses was out of step with the Law of God, and that was why Jesus objected to it.

> They said to him, 'Why then did Moses command us to give a certificate of dismissal and to divorce her?' He said to them, 'It was because you were so hard-hearted that Moses allowed you to divorce your wives, but from the beginning it was not so'. (Matthew 19:7-8)

151

> From the very beginning of the Church there have been men and women who have renounced the great good of marriage to follow the Lamb wherever he goes, to be intent on the things of the Lord, to seek to please him, and to go out to meet the Bridegroom who is coming. (CCC 1618)

A young Irish medical student went to work during her summer holidays in an orphanage in Moldova. The conditions were very poor, so when she returned to Ireland she decided to interrupt her studies in order to work among the young orphans she had come to love so much. When she told her family she was leaving them, they were upset at her strange action, but they supported her in her brave decision.

Jesus once did something very like this. He was a Jew, and family was central to Jewish life. But he had no wife or children of his own. In fact, he left his own family to devote himself to God and God's people. In a strange way, he thereby gained a much larger family. The single man with no wife or children became the bridegroom of the whole human race, and every person on earth became his brother or sister.

> As the bridegroom was delayed, all of them became drowsy and slept. But at midnight there was a shout, 'Look! Here is the bridegroom! Come out to meet him.' Then all those bridesmaids got up and trimmed their lamps. (Matthew 25:2-7)

> Authentic married love is caught up into divine love. (CCC 1639)

At the marriage of David and Melissa in Balheary Church, I spoke about the three readings they had selected for their Wedding Mass. Each reading touched on an important aspect of love. The Song of Songs text exulted in the sexual and erotic love between man and woman. The text from St Paul spoke about the practical and caring aspects of friendship and love of neighbour. The Gospel text spoke about God binding each married couple together as one.

Clearly the couple beginning married life want to be erotic and careful lovers at one and the same time. Wedding bells celebrate all these riches to be found in human sexual love. But they also rejoice in an even deeper love – the love at the very heart of God's inner life, a love called 'agape'. This love pours out from God into the world to make it live; this love pours out from God in a very special way into the hearts of all people who come together in marriage.

> Beloved, let us love one another, because love is from God; everyone who loves is born of God and knows God. Whoever does not love does not know God, for God is love. (1 John 4:7-8)

> By its very nature conjugal love requires the inviolable fidelity of the spouses. This is the consequence of the gift of themselves which they make to each other. Love seeks to be definitive; it cannot be an arrangement 'until further notice'. (CCC 1646)

Would you Believe? deals with a wide range of complex human and religious issues. It featured a wife looking after a sick husband at home for a quarter of a century. In his early forties he had been diagnosed with Alzheimer's; this condition is incurable, and his needs are such that he requires twenty-four hour care. Rather than sending him elsewhere, she has decided to care for him at home.

When asked why she is willing to do this, she speaks quietly about her marriage vows: 'For better and for worse, in sickness and in health'. She regards what she is doing for her sick husband as part of her life commitment. Her faith in God is clear: looking at her husband, she knows he his content where he is, and unwilling yet to cast off the mortal coil. Her physician claims that the husband's longevity is very unusual, and probably connected to the care he receives.

> Love is patient; love is kind; love is not envious or boastful or arrogant or rude. It does not insist on its own way; it is not irritable or resentful; it does not rejoice in wrongdoing, but rejoices in the truth. It bears all things, believes all things, hopes all things, endures all things. (1 Corinthians 13:4-7)

> Children are the supreme gift of marriage and contribute greatly to the good of the parents themselves. (CCC 1652)

My neighbour Paddy's grandson – Ronan, who was just three at the time – almost drowned. His mother lost sight of him for barely a second, during which he leapt into a swimming pool. Rushed to hospital, his condition was very serious; he was unconscious and nobody knew how things might develop. Paddy asked us to pray for him and we did, but there was an air of depression about the place. Then Paddy began to smile – the news was good. Ronan had regained consciousness and there was no brain damage.

Parents love their children and want only the best for them. When illness strikes or accidents occur, parents know real pain. Feeling responsible for their child's welfare, but sensing the frustration of being unable to protect them always, parents know the crucifying shape of true love. As Jesus needed Simon to help him carry his cross, parents need friends to hold them aloft when tragedy strikes. Prayer can be a true support.

> When his parents saw him they were astonished; and his mother said to him, 'Child, why have you treated us like this? Look, your father and I have been searching for you in great anxiety.' He said to them, 'Why were you searching for me? Did you not know that I must be in my Father's house?' But they did not understand what he said to them. (Luke 2:48-50)

> A farewell to the deceased is his final 'commendation to God' by the Church. It is the last farewell by which the Christian community greets one of its members before his body is brought to its tomb'. The Byzantine tradition expresses this by the kiss of farewell to the deceased. (CCC 1690)

The Gospel today is stark in its simplicity: be ready for the coming of the Son of Man. Jesus warned his disciples to be prepared for death, because nobody knows the day nor the hour. Death is a serious business – it is a moment in which we sum up the entire thrust of our lives on earth. It is truly a crisis moment. Taking with us all we have become, we enter into the next life and face the hidden future there. Of course, this does not mean we ought to be frightened of death. For Jesus comes not only as judge but also as saviour. He has gone through death himself; he knows its mystery from within. He will join us in our death and lead us by the hand safely home to heaven.

Once again sudden death was in the news. A Romanian immigrant found dead in a suitcase in the Royal Canal was waked. He is the only son of his mother, who came to receive his remains and bring them back home for burial. The Orthodox Community in Dublin, many of whom are from Romania, gathered in their church in Arbour Hill to remember their dead brother and commend his soul to God. His mother brought with her a new suit of clothes in which he was buried.

> For since we believe that Jesus died and rose again, even so, through Jesus, God wil bring with him those who have died. (1 Thessalonians 4:14)

PART THREE

Life in Christ

The Dignity of the Human Person

> The dignity of the human person is rooted in his creation in the image and likeness of God. (CCC 1700)

A scientist in the USA, from an analysis of the mitochondrial DNA of a variety of people of diverse ethnic groups all over the world, claims that all the earth's people outside Africa share a common female ancestor. If this claim proves to be true, it would have very interesting moral implications. Above all, it would mean that humans of all kinds and colours and shapes and sizes belong to one very large extended family.

This conviction has been at the heart of the Jewish and Christian religions, who argue from their foundational belief in a creator God to the unity of the human family created in God's image and likeness. In spite of this religious conviction, however, there have been many occasions when actions of believers did not reflect their belief, when some people were regarded as inferior to others, and when difference was confused with superior value. Especially at a time of war, humans need to remember who they are.

> Then God said, 'Let us make humankind in our image, according to our likeness'. (Genesis 1:26)

> The Beatitudes are at the heart of Jesus' preaching. They take up the promises made to the chosen people since Abraham. (CCC 1716)

On the anniversary of James Joyce's walking out with Nora Barnacle, his fans celebrate Bloomsday. Some walk along Sandymount Strand; others follow the route of Paddy Dignam's funeral through the centre of the city out as far as Glasnevin. I had Dublin Jews on my mind when my car stopped in traffic at Fairview. The house to my right had a small plaque: 'Built in the year 5618'.

This is not a mistake; the house was once home to Jews, and this is their way of calculating time. Jews have a strong sense of God the Creator, who made the world and all within it, and then called them to be his special people charged with living a godly life in God's world. Jews are the older family members of we who follow Jesus the Jew, and much of our spirituality is derived from theirs.

> Blessed are the poor in spirit, for theirs is the kingdom of heaven. Blessed are those who mourn, for they will be comforted. Blessed are the meek, for they will inherit the earth. Blessed are those who hunger and thirst for righteousness, for they will be filled. (Matthew 5:3-6)

> The Beatitudes depict the countenance of Jesus Christ and portray his charity ... they shed light on the actions and attitudes characteristic of the Christian life. (CCC 1717)

While reading the Beatitudes before Mass today, I could only smile at the irony of it all. Everything that is prized in modern life is given the 'thumbs down': wealth, aggression and assertiveness in particular. These values, which give meaning to the lives of so many people, are shown to be inadequate in the human search for true happiness and a blessed experience. Instead, the values lived by Jesus, and (it is hoped) by his followers are commended to all and sundry.

To be poor in spirit, to mourn for the wrongs of the world, to be firm without aggression, to hunger and thirst passionately for justice, to show mercy even when it is undeserved, to be pure of heart, to work for peace and to face persecution with courage – such are the distinguishing marks of Jesus himself. Consequently, they must be the marks of all who believe in him and claim to be his followers.

> Blessed are the merciful, for they will receive mercy. Blessed are the pure in heart, for they will see God. Blessed are the peacemakers, for they will be called children of God. Blessed are those who are persecuted for righteousness' sake, for theirs is the kingdom of heaven. (Matthew 5:7-10)

> Freedom makes man responsible for his acts to the extent that they are voluntary. (CCC 1734)

Robert Holohan, a boy of barely eleven, was missing for about a week – then his body was found. The shock experienced by his family has been palpable, and yet it has been lessened by the support given by hundreds of ordinary folk who came to east Cork to join in the search. Then a local newspaper compounds the tragedy by the very words it chooses to describe it.

But what is meant by naming the killer as a monster, then calling for him to be put in prison and asking that the key be thrown away? Whoever committed this crime is indeed guilty of very serious wrongdoing, but he remains a human being, in spite of the fact that he has taken the life of an innocent one. Can we not accept that fact? It is one of us, not an outsider or monster, who has done this terrible deed.

> Cain said to his brother Abel, 'Let us go out to the field.' And when they were in the field, Cain rose up against his brother Abel, and killed him. Then the LORD said to Cain, 'Where is your brother Abel?' He said, 'I do not know; am I my brother's keeper?' (Genesis 4:8-9)

> There are acts which, in and of themselves, independently of circumstances and intentions, are always gravely illicit by reason of their object; such as blasphemy and perjury, murder and adultery. (CCC 1756)

When reading *Macbeth* in school years ago, I remember being very affected by the unfolding tragedy. Old King Duncan visits Macbeth's castle, where he expects to be well cared for by one of his leading generals. However, Lady Macbeth and her husband conspire to have the king murdered in his sleep. This is not simply violence, but ingratitude and treason as well. The raven croaks an ode to death.

Michael and James were two young Irish farmers, whose short lives both ended in tragedy. Michael felt very aggrieved at losing part of the family farm, in which he had invested so much time and energy. James had bought this land from Michael's sister, who had gained this share of the property because her parents made no will. When James was trying to fence off his land, Michael shot him dead. Later the same day he shot himself. Two families are now united in grief.

> In the morning David wrote a letter to Joab, and sent it by the hand of Uriah. In the letter he wrote, 'Set Uriah in the forefront of the hardest fighting, and then draw back from him, so that he may be struck down and die.' As Joab was besieging the city, he assigned Uriah to the place where he knew there were valiant warriors. The men of the city came out and fought with Joab; and some of the servants of David among the people fell. Uriah the Hittite was killed as well. (2 Samuel 11:14-17)

> His conscience is man's most secret core and his sanctuary. There he is alone with God whose voice echoes in his depths. (CCC 1776)

Forty years ago Brian Friel wrote his first play, *Philadelphia, Here I Come*. It's a moving portrayal of the debate going on in the heart of Gar, a young man in a rural Irish village, on the evening before he leaves home to go to the USA. The pluses and minuses of going or staying are placed in the balance, and they are weighed with much humour and insight. We never find out whether he eventually went or stayed.

A memorable aspect of the play is the way Gar is played by two actors: 'Public Gar' and 'Private Gar'. One might even call them 'The Gar you see' and 'The Gar you don't', or even 'Gar' and his 'Conscience'. This fascinating technique allows complex human motivation, feeling and reasoning processes to be simplified and clarified. The tragedy at work in Gar's family and communal life brought tears to my eyes.

> When Gentiles, who do not possess the law, do instinctively what the law requires, these, though not having the law, are a law to themselves. They show that what the law requires is written on their hearts, to which their own conscience also bears witness; and their conflicting thoughts will accuse or perhaps excuse them on the day when, according to my gospel, God, through Jesus Christ, will judge the secret thoughts of all. (Romans 2:14-16)

> Moral conscience, present at the heart of the person, enjoins him at the appropriate moment to do good and to avoid evil. It also judges particular choices, approving those that are good and denouncing those that are evil. (CCC 1777)

Two smiling faces graced our TV screens. One belonged to Amrozi bin Nurhasyim, a forty-year-old just sentenced to death in Indonesia for his part in the Bali bombings that killed over two hundred people. It seemed he was very proud of his activities; he even smiled at the relatives of those whom he had killed. There is a belief in some Islamic circles that if you die while fighting in God's good cause, you are guaranteed heaven. Was that his belief?

The other smiling face belonged to John Gilligan, a notorious Irish drug dealer, whose efforts had just failed to have his jail sentence quashed. He had also been charged with the murder of Veronica Guerin, but this was not proved. Now he faces nearly thirty years in jail. Does he have no sense of the evil he committed while selling harmful drugs to addicts? Does he have no feeling in his heart for the relatives and friends of those who died from drug overdoses? Where is human decency? Has conscience died entirely?

> While Paul was looking intently at the council he said, 'Brothers, up to this day I have lived my life with a clear conscience before God'. (Acts 23:1)

> The education of the conscience is a lifelong task
> ... [It] guarantees freedom and engenders peace of
> heart. (CCC 1784)

How do you give advice to someone burdened with a
moral problem? This was what we explored in a
workshop on the Good School. Help her to clarify the
values at stake in the dilemma that confronts her. Get
her to take responsibility for her own life and stop
worrying about what friends may think. Tell her to cop
on and stop lying to her parents. Point out to her that
she has already made many good moral decisions and
shouldn't fear the burden of new ones.

These, and many other suggestions, were articulated.
Underneath each piece of advice, of course, is a set of
assumptions about what constitutes the heart of moral
living. We decided to unearth these assumptions at our
next gathering. All of this is related to our belief that a
Good School should foster moral maturity among the
pupils. Helping young people to grow up morally is a
noble vocation.

> Then Jesus said to the Jews who had believed in
> him, 'If you continue in my word, you are truly
> my disciples; and you will know the truth, and the
> truth will make you free'. (John 8:31-32)

> In the formation of conscience the Word of God is
> the light for our path ... We must also examine our
> conscience before the Lord's Cross. We are assisted
> by the gifts of the Holy Spirit, aided by the witness
> or advice of others and guided by the authoritative
> teaching of the Church. (CCC 1785)

Linda Hogan's book about conscience in the Catholic
Tradition is very appositely entitled *Confronting the
Truth*. It has always been a firm conviction of the
Catholic Church that the Holy Spirit is poured upon her
in order to lead her into the whole truth. Clearly this
implies that there will be a long, and often insecure,
journey to be made before the truth is fully revealed.
Looking back over the history of the Church, it is clear
that we have very quickly grasped some elements of
moral truth, while others have been very slow to emerge.

It is good to celebrate the Church's positive
appropriation of such moral values as respect for human
life or global justice and peace. However, the Church's
record on slavery or usury or religious freedom is not
good. The development of humanity's conscience in
regard to these issues owes more to factors outside than
inside the Church. Yet we also believe the Holy Spirit
blows where he wills.

> How sweet are your words to my taste, sweeter
> than honey to my mouth! Through your precepts I
> get understanding; therefore I hate every false
> way. Your word is a lamp to my feet and a light to
> my path. (Psalms 119:103-105)

> Prudence is the virtue that disposes practical reason to discern our true good in every circumstance and to choose the right means of achieving it. (CCC 1806)

A boating accident took place near Fethard-on-Sea. A small fishing boat sank about a mile from shore, and though a few people were saved, most of the passengers were drowned. The saddest case of all was surely one local woman who lost her father, her husband and one of her sons. When all the dead bodies were recovered, the boat was salvaged from the seabed and experts tried to explain what went wrong.

The most worrying aspect of this tragedy is the fact that nobody on board was wearing a life jacket. One assumes that normal safety precautions ought to have been routine on all fishing boats. Why not on this one? Who is responsible for the omission? What lessons will be learnt from this sad occurrence? Human life is too great a blessing to be treated recklessly and without due care.

> My child, do not let these escape from your sight: keep sound wisdom and prudence, and they will be life for your soul and adornment for your neck. Then you will walk on your way securely and your foot will not stumble. (Proverbs 3:21-23)

> Fortitude is the moral virtue that ensures firmness in difficulties and constancy in the pursuit of the good. (CCC 1808)

A programme on the BBC tries to evoke the horrors of trench warfare during World War I. It brings a group of 'conscripts' from England to northern France where trenches have been preserved and, following the record of surviving diaries, puts them through the routine life of a soldier at war. The boredom of daily life is regularly shattered by the threat of attack and the fear that envelops every heart.

While recognising the bravery of the original soldiers who fought and died in their millions, we should always remember that war is not the only arena for bravery to shine. Everybody is confronted at least now and again with challenges that require a brave spirit. To name injustice, to pursue the wrongdoer and to call on authority to do its duty are hard for most people to do. Only the brave are free to act.

> I was pushed hard, so that I was falling, but the LORD helped me. The LORD is my strength and my might; he has become my salvation. (Psalms 118:13-14)

> The disciple of Christ must not only keep the faith and live on it, but also profess it, confidently bear witness to it and spread it: 'All ... must be prepared to confess Christ before men and to follow him along the way of the Cross, amidst the persecutions which the Church never lacks'. (CCC 1816)

We know very little about St Mark, but his memory is very strong among the Coptic Christians in Egypt and in the beautiful city of Venice. Tradition has it that he was the scribe of St Peter, and that his Gospel represents the editing of the notes he took while listening to Peter's sermons. Another story identifies Mark with the young man who ran away naked from the Garden of Gethsemane after seeing the betrayal of Jesus.

St Mark's Gospel tells of the challenges that confront the true disciple of Christ. In a nutshell, faith must pass through death to new life. There is no Easter glory without the desolation of the Cross. This Gospel is the shortest of all. I love the way it reveals the emotional life of Jesus, and also how it says things so simply, with little elaboration, allowing the listener to use one's imagination.

> So do not be afraid; you are of more value than many sparrows. Everyone therefore who acknowledges me before others, I also will acknowledge before my Father in heaven; but whoever denies me before others, I also will deny before my Father in heaven. (Matthew 10:31-33)

Hope is expressed and nourished in prayer, especially in the Our Father, the summary of everything that hope leads us to desire. (CCC 1820)

We visited the Basilica of St Paul's outside the Walls (of Rome). This is where Paul was laid to rest after being beheaded as a martyr. People like us have been gathering around the burial places of martyrs since the very early days of the Church in Rome. They have come to pay their respects and to pray and draw spiritual nourishment from the witness given by these brave people.

Not far from St Paul's is the Catacomb of St Domitilla. In our underground journey through the burial place of hundreds of early Christians, we learned about the two soldiers whose conversion led to their execution, and also about the banishment suffered by the wealthy Domitilla after her conversion to Christ. Belief in Jesus Christ regularly leads to suffering or even death, but such a death is simply the passage to a new risen life with God. Catacombs are places of hope as well as centres of death. God raises up the lowly, and the lowliest of course are the dead.

Rejoice in hope, be patient in suffering, persevere in prayer. (Romans 12:12)

> Charity is the theological virtue by which we love God above all things for his own sake, and our neighbour as ourselves for the love of God. (CCC 1822)

The house in Kerry has served us well for over twenty years. Though a long way from Dublin, it provides a very comfortable retreat in a beautiful location. We named it *Gort an Oir* (the golden field) because it is in Gortadoo (the black fields) and not far from Fort del Oro (the golden fort). One of the prettiest beaches imaginable, Béal Bán (the white mouth), is within ten or fifteen minutes' walk.

When we are absent our great neighbour, Páid Moriarty, looks after the premises. But poor Páid has cancer and is fading fast. They say he will hardly last the coming months. His family will miss him dearly, but so will all who have been warmed by his infectious smile. Good neighbours are better than gold. When they die, we feel diminished. Life is rich when we can rely on caring people to attend to our needs.

> As the Father has loved me, so I have loved you; abide in my love. If you keep my commandments, you will abide in my love, just as I have kept my Father's commandments and abide in his love. I have said these things to you so that my joy may be in you, and that your joy may be complete. This is my commandment, that you love one another as I have loved you. No one has greater love than this, to lay down one's life for one's friends. (John 15:9-13)

> The seven gifts of the Holy Spirit are wisdom, understanding, counsel, fortitude, knowledge, piety and fear of the Lord. (CCC 1831)

During a planning meeting for Confirmation in the North Inner City Deanery, the question is asked about the link between the pledge and Confirmation. We discover that the vast majority of the girls preparing for the sacrament are aware of the evils of drug addiction and see a positive value in pledging to not abuse drugs. Quite a number are already drinking alcohol and see no sense in pledging not to drink.

One of the gifts of the Holy Spirit at Confirmation is wisdom. As a nation, we clearly need the wisdom to recognise that alcohol is a drug (even though legally available). We also need the knowledge that alcohol-related illnesses and deaths far outnumber those connected with illegal drugs. Above all else, we need the courage to make the hard decision when we receive little social support.

> A shoot shall come out from the stump of Jesse, and a branch shall grow out of his roots. The spirit of the LORD shall rest on him, the spirit of wisdom and understanding, the spirit of counsel and might, the spirit of knowledge and the fear of the LORD. (Isaiah 11:1-2)

> Sin is an offence against reason, truth and right conscience; it is failure in genuine love for God and neighbour caused by a perverse attachment to certain goods. (CCC 1849)

The Co-Cathedral of St John the Baptist in Valletta is where all the Grand Masters of the Order of St John are buried. Their burial pavements fill the entire nave of the church. The most interesting aspect of the building is that there are chapels dedicated to the various nations (*langues*), which used to provide knights for the Order. Long before the EU became a reality, the Order of St John provided a kind of preview of European co-operation in the field of health.

Even good ideas can come to naught. In spite of the spirit of international co-operation, the normal international rivalries often came to the fore, with one nation trying to outdo another through the magnificence of its paintings and sculptures. Through time, the Order once established to care for the sick itself became sick to the core, as it grew in wealth and political power.

> *To the leader. A Psalm of David, when the prophet Nathan came to him, after he had gone in to Bathsheba.*

> Have mercy on me, O God, according to your steadfast love; according to your abundant mercy blot out my transgressions. Wash me thoroughly from my iniquity, and cleanse me from my sin. For I know my transgressions, and my sin is ever before me. Against you, you alone, have I sinned, and done what is evil in your sight, so that you are justified in your sentence and blameless when you pass judgement. (Psalms 51:1-4)

> Mortal sin destroys charity in the heart of man by a
> grave violation of God's law; it turns man away from
> God, who is his ultimate end and his beatitude, by
> preferring an inferior good to him. (CCC 1855)

At the end of one of J.B. Keane's tragedies, the
simpleton, Neelus Conlee, carries his crippled cousin,
Dinzie Conlee, on his back out of the house and jumps
with him into the sea-cave, called *Sharon's Grave*.
Neelus, though weak in mind, is wholesome and
humane. Dinzie, whose disadvantages are purely
physical, has allowed himself become bitter, aggressive,
calculating and evil. Seldom have I seen on stage such a
riveting portrayal of human depravity.

When Keane first submitted his play, *Sharon's Grave*, the
Abbey refused to accept it, because of its evocation of
the wildness of the Irish psyche, especially that
all-consuming lust for land and power, which is the
driving force behind many family feuds and community
battles. 'The truth is bitter', according to the old Irish
saying. What did Keane mean in that dramatic last
scene, by so uniting the good and evil characters that
they formed one persona, which then ran off into
oblivion?

> If you see your brother or sister committing what
> is not a mortal sin, you will ask, and God will give
> life to such a one – to those whose sin is not
> mortal. There is sin that is mortal; I do not say that
> you should pray about that. All wrongdoing is sin,
> but there is sin that is not mortal. (1 John 5:16-17)

> Sin creates a proclivity to sin; it engenders vice by repetition of the same acts. This results in perverse inclinations which cloud conscience and corrupt the concrete judgement of good and evil. (CCC 1865)

Tracy Chevalier's first novel is called *The Virgin Blue*. The action takes place mainly in the south of France and in Switzerland, while the timescale alternates between the sixteenth and the twentieth centuries. There are strange parallels between the two main characters, Ella Turner and Isabelle du Moulin. Blue and red are major factors in the development of the plot. *The Virgin Blue* evokes the Catholic style of representing Mary in art.

As the novel unfolds, we enter the religious wars that led to death and persecution for many French Protestants. The Calvinist preachers of the Truth and the Counter Reformation Catholic clergy are now in the ascendancy and then in decline. Ethnic cleansing takes place; thousands flee for their lives to safe havens far from home. This novel is a sad reflection on the sinfulness of religious people.

> O LORD, how long shall the wicked, how long shall the wicked exult? They pour out their arrogant words; all the evildoers boast. They crush your people, O LORD, and afflict your heritage. They kill the widow and the stranger, they murder the orphan, and they say, 'The LORD does not see; the God of Jacob does not perceive'. (Psalms 94:3-7)

'Structures of sin' are the expression and effect of personal sins. They lead their victims to do evil in their turn. In an analogous sense, they constitute a 'social sin'. (CCC 1869)

One of the least glamorous works of mercy is visiting prisoners. The organisation known as Kairos had been doing pastoral work in English prisons for years, but it eventually met with serious opposition from some government officials. In many societies there is no clear consensus about the main function of prison – is it to protect society from convicted criminals, or is it to help these unfortunates to regain some dignity so that they can reintegrate into society when they leave prison?

Governor John Lonergan of Mountjoy Gaol constantly refers to the fact that the vast majority of the prisoners in his care come from a small number of precise locations in the cities of Ireland. Their becoming criminals is predictable, given their place of origin. How is this possible? Are not all people guaranteed equality before the law? Why does the law punish some communities more extensively than others?

> Listen! The wages of the labourers who mowed your fields, which you kept back by fraud, cry out, and the cries of the harvesters have reached the ears of the Lord of hosts. You have lived on the earth in luxury and in pleasure; you have fattened your hearts in a day of slaughter. You have condemned and murdered the righteous one, who does not resist you. (James 5:4-6)

The Human Community

> The human person needs to live in society. (CCC 1879)

One of my greatest sources of regular enjoyment is being part of two book circles. The earlier one (started in 1977) is for the reading of theological books. This attracts seven or eight priests once a month. The second one (started in 1983) is for the reading of general literature, usually novels, but sometimes historical or scientific works. The participants here are a group of school pals and their spouses, who get together regularly – some even come in from abroad.

'Not on bread alone does man live'. We all need other food: food for the mind, food for the imagination and food for the heart. But beyond this obvious food, we also need the excitement of sharing thoughts, ideas, questions and complaints in a friendly and respectful environment. If ever there was proof needed that people live in the shadow of each other, if ever evidence was sought for the human search for community, book circles like these would be among the prime exhibits.

> He summoned ten of his slaves, and gave them ten pounds, and said to them, 'Do business with these until I come back.' When he returned, having received royal power, he ordered these slaves, to whom he had given the money, to be summoned so that he might find out what they had gained by trading. (Luke 19:13, 15)

> Where sin has perverted the social climate, it is necessary to call for the conversion of hearts and appeal to the grace of God. Charity urges just reforms. (CCC 1896)

Irish Politicians have come under fire because some of them allegedly took bribes. Bishops all over Ireland have been accused of cynical disregard for sexually abused children. Lawyers are regularly pilloried for seeking inflated payments for their work. Now a new Tribunal opens in Donegal, and allegations are made that certain members of the Police Force (An Garda Síochána) killed a man and attempted to blame others for their crime.

All the pillars of Irish society are in the dock. Respect for the institutions of Church and State seems to be lessening all the time. Are these institutions ready to accept fair criticism and make the necessary changes? Or will they challenge the evidence and contest the truth of the allegations? Irish society is at a crossroads. For centuries Irish people resisted injustice from Britain – how well will Ireland combat home-produced wrongdoing?

> Then he began to reproach the cities in which most of his deeds of power had been done, because they did not repent. 'Woe to you, Chorazin! Woe to you, Bethsaida! For if the deeds of power done in you had been done in Tyre and Sidon, they would have repented long ago in sackcloth and ashes'. (Matthew 11:20-21)

> Authority is exercised legitimately only when it seeks the common good of the group concerned and if it employs morally licit means to attain it. (CCC 1903)

The Dublin Archdiocese came under close scrutiny in a *Prime Time* special, which dealt with clerical sex abuse and the way it was handled by the diocesan authorities. The pain felt by many victims of abuse was magnified by the allegedly poor response to their requests for help. Known abusive priests were reassigned to work in other parishes, which gave them new opportunities for the abuse of children.

Many questions still remain. In particular, there is the issue of the criminal nature of the sin of abuse. Can the Church insist it wants to deal only with the sin of the priest and neglect to tell the civil authority that a crime has been committed? On the other hand, while accepting the values of openness and transparency, can the Church neglect the value of confidentiality? And is Dublin truly the worst in the world, with over four hundred abuse cases still outstanding in the courts?

> For the Lord's sake accept the authority of every human institution, whether of the emperor as supreme, or of governors, as sent by him to punish those who do wrong and to praise those who do right. For it is God's will that by doing right you should silence the ignorance of the foolish. As servants of God, live as free people, yet do not use your freedom as a pretext for evil. Honour everyone. Love the family of believers. Fear God. Honour the emperor. (1 Peter 2:13-17)

> Social justice can be obtained only in respecting the transcendent dignity of man. The person represents the ultimate end of society, which is ordered to him. (CCC 1929)

All the references in CRED are to the *Catechism of the Catholic Church*, which runs to about seven hundred pages. This kind of large catechism has always been accompanied by smaller books, which offer a more concise presentation of the faith. I read one recently by Herbert McCabe called *The Teaching of the Catholic Church*. It follows the question and answer style first made popular by Martin Luther. McCabe's Question 230 is, 'How is justice exercised in the Church?'

His answer runs as follows: 'Justice is exercised in the Church by practical concern for those groups which may not yet have sufficient official voice in the Church, notably the laity and women: by the efficient and speedy despatch of legal justice, especially in marriage cases, and by respect for legitimate freedom of opinion within the Church'. Here is a prophet, drawing upon the highly respected social teaching of the Church and applying it directly to her inner life.

> Then they also will answer, 'Lord, when was it that we saw you hungry or thirsty or a stranger or naked or sick or in prison, and did not take care of you?' Then he will answer them, 'Truly I tell you, just as you did not do it to one of the least of these, you did not do it to me.' And these will go away into eternal punishment, but the righteous into eternal life. (Matthew 25:44-46)

> The equality of men rests essentially on their dignity as persons and the rights that flow from it. (CCC 1935)

The Known World, by Edward P. Jones, is a novel that explores the lives of slaves in southern USA before the Civil War. Many of us judged its style unattractive, because there were so many people and one could be easily confused, and the author often looked to the future as well as the past, so at times one wondered where the action was taking place. These problems, however, could not take away from its overall riveting evocation of slavery.

Two ideas remain with me: the first is the extent to which black American freed slaves themselves became masters of other slaves; the second was the acceptance by society of the normality of possessing slaves. If a slave ran away, not only was he an outlaw, but he was also regarded as a thief – he had effectively stolen his master's property (himself) and could be further punished for this crime.

> Perhaps this is the reason he was separated from you for a while, so that you might have him back forever, no longer as a slave but more than a slave, a beloved brother – especially to me but how much more to you, both in the flesh and in the Lord. So if you consider me your partner, welcome him as you would welcome me. If he has wronged you in any way, or owes you anything, charge that to my account. (Philemon 1:15-18)

> Solidarity is manifested in the first place by the distribution of goods and remuneration for work. (CCC 1940)

Irish people well remember times of massive unemployment, when millions of our relatives and friends had to go abroad in search of work. With our booming economy, we now depend on workers from abroad to fill many jobs in Ireland. Who would have thought that Turkey would supply so many to our construction industry? Had not our navvies built the roads and tunnels of England? Enter GAMA Construction Ireland, and the issue of poorly paid migrants is in the news.

Thank God the news media have highlighted the problems: grown men reduced to eating bread and olives, and afraid they will be put out of their accommodation by the weekend. Whatever the rights and wrongs of this case, economically and politically, the humanitarian issue must remain central. Jesus taught that, 'as often as you neglect to do it to one of these, the least of my brothers, you fail to do it to me'. Many Irish people, thank God, still subscribe to this.

> Religion that is pure and undefiled before God, the Father, is this: to care for orphans and widows in their distress, and to keep oneself unstained by the world. (James 1:27)

God's Salvation: Law and Grace

> Called to beatitude but wounded by sin, man stands in need of salvation from God. Divine help comes to him in Christ through the law that guides him and the grace that sustains him. (CCC 1949)

The electricity of God's love and forgiveness is constantly flowing through the universe. But it doesn't touch us automatically. It can stay hidden from us, unavailable to us. To avail ourselves of this power we have to switch it on. This we do by opening up to God in faith, hope and love. Will many be saved? We simply do not know. What we do know is that God wants everybody to be saved, even murderers, even rapists.

Salvation means living with God's life coursing through our veins, and God's love and forgiveness influencing our every thought, word and deed. Salvation can begin in this life, but it will be complete only in the next. The Good News of Jesus is that God is truly on our side and wants to save us. But equally Jesus reminds us that we remain free – free even to turn our backs on this generous offer. We can refuse God's gift of salvation. That is the mystery of human perversity. From such a disaster, protect us all, oh Lord.

> Therefore, my beloved, just as you have always obeyed me, not only in my presence, but much more now in my absence, work out your own salvation with fear and trembling; for it is God who is at work in you, enabling you both to will and to work for his good pleasure. (Philippians 2:12-13)

> The New Law practises the acts of religion: almsgiving, prayer and fasting. (CCC 1969)

The Catholic bishops of Ireland invited us to do something very concrete in response to the tragedy in Asia. Firstly, we are to gather together in a spirit of reflection to pray for the dead and for those suffering. Being children of the same Heavenly Father makes this an easy task to accomplish. The bishops have also asked us to fast, as a gesture of solidarity with those who are hungry. We are encouraged to deny ourselves some food, in order to be more at one with those who have no choice about being hungry.

The third thing we are asked to do is contribute generously to those who have nothing. This is, perhaps, the aspect that will get most attention in the media. But for people of faith, such almsgiving is merely the flower on the stem of fasting that is rooted in deep prayer. From our gazing at God (in child-like prayer) comes delight in our own blessings, which we are then willing to let go (fasting) so as to be generous with others (alms).

> So whenever you give alms, do not sound a trumpet before you, as the hypocrites do in the synagogues and in the streets, so that they may be praised by others. Truly I tell you, they have received their reward. But when you give alms, do not let your left hand know what your right hand is doing, so that your alms may be done in secret; and your Father who sees in secret will reward you. (Matthew 5:2-4)

> To the Lord's Sermon on the Mount it is fitting to add the moral catechesis of the apostolic teachings, such as ... Contribute to the needs of the saints, practise hospitality. (CCC 1971)

When I heard the doorbell ringing late in the evening, I went to check it out. She stood straight up, while he lounged against the lobby. I was just about to tell them that Liam was not there, when she remarked that Liam had spoken to her on the phone a few minutes earlier and had asked her to come to the house. Liam emerged from upstairs, his phone in hand, and invited them both in. I went to watch the news.

In a few moments the pair joined me. Liam was still busy and would look after them shortly. I saw they were both very dirty and guessed from their accents that they were travellers. Each was smoking and there was no ashtray. I suggested they could use the bin in the kitchen. Some words passed between us, but I was very tired and began to snooze. I was not a very welcoming host.

> Let love be genuine; hate what is evil, hold fast to what is good; love one another with mutual affection; outdo one another in showing honour. Do not lag in zeal, be ardent in spirit, serve the Lord. Rejoice in hope, be patient in suffering, persevere in prayer. Contribute to the needs of the saints; extend hospitality to strangers. (Romans 12:9-13)

> Justification has been merited for us by the Passion of Christ who offered himself on the cross as a living victim, holy and pleasing to God, and whose blood has become the instrument of atonement for the sins of all men. (CCC 1992)

It was a very unusual museum visit. Michael assembled us under the shade of a pine tree before he led us in, and told us there was only one single item in the museum that we were going to see. We were all excited to know what it was. He told us it had been found twenty years ago during excavations in Rome's Palatine Hill. Now it was on display, but very few people had ever heard about it.

As we stood before it, Michael explained it was hard to see it properly. But he gave us some help and we eventually saw it. It was a small square of plaster with a number of irregular lines drawn by a bad artist – second century graffiti. However, then we noticed the two vertical human legs, the two horizontal stick-arms and above them the head of a donkey; a man bowed before it in adoration. Here was a very early pagan image of the crucifixion: a Christian worshipping his God (an ass).

> Since all have sinned and fall short of the glory of God; they are now justified by his grace as a gift, through the redemption that is in Christ Jesus, whom God put forward as a sacrifice of atonement by his blood, effective through faith. He did this to show his righteousness, because in his divine forbearance he had passed over the sins previously committed; it was to prove at the present time that he himself is righteous and that he justifies the one who has faith in Jesus. (Romans 3:23-25)

> Grace is a participation in the life of God. It introduces us into the intimacy of Trinitarian life. (CCC 1997)

The feast of the Immaculate Conception celebrates the great things that God, the almighty one, has done for Mary. By preserving her free from sin from the first moment of her existence, God has revealed two very important truths: one, that divine life is graciousness poured out; and two, that humanity at its best is grace-filled and sinless. When we meet sin, we often comment, 'Sure it's only human'. The humanity of sin is not humanity at its best, it is simply humanity in search of life.

We are invited today to give thanks for what God has done for Mary, by way of privilege, and also for what Jesus is, by nature, as Son of God. To call someone 'sinless' is to use a poor term for being full of grace. Mary's grace *from God* and Jesus' grace *as God* are also available to us, as long as we open our hearts to God's Holy Spirit. God continues to offer to us today what he has revealed in Jesus and what he has given specially to Mary: a share in God's intimate life.

> For all who are led by the Spirit of God are children of God. For you did not receive a spirit of slavery to fall back into fear, but you have received a spirit of adoption. When we cry, 'Abba! Father!' it is that very Spirit bearing witness with our spirit that we are children of God, and if children, then heirs, heirs of God and joint heirs with Christ – if, in fact, we suffer with him so that we may also be glorified with him. (Romans 8:4-17)

> All Christians in any state or walk of life are called to the fullness of Christian life and to the perfection of charity. All are called to holiness. (CCC 2013)

Jesus invited his followers to become the salt of the earth and the light of the world. Not everybody has reached these high levels, and there is often a cry for repentance. But today the cry is one of celebration – one is entitled to rejoice that so many ordinary folk actually do reach these standards of excellence. The Gospel has indeed taken root in many souls and brought forth many lively and beautiful fruits.

The person who reaches out a hand to help when floods invade your house; the person who speaks to the foreigner even when he doesn't understand their language; the person whose smile makes you feel welcome and at home; the person who sees your needs even before you notice them yourself – such are the lights of this world, such are the salt of the earth. And everybody knows at least a few, thank God.

> For if you love those who love you, what reward do you have? Do not even the tax collectors do the same? And if you greet only your brothers and sisters, what more are you doing than others? Do not even the Gentiles do the same? Be perfect, therefore, as your heavenly Father is perfect. (Matthew 5:46-48)

> Sanctifying grace is the gratuitous gift of his life that God makes to us; it is infused by the Holy Spirit into the soul to heal it of sin and to sanctify it. (CCC 2023)

Who are the goodies and who are the baddies? This is the question behind most fairy tales and the topic of many novels and films. We automatically categorise people into good and bad, though often the basis of our judgement is little more than our own private likes or dislikes. Sometimes we have more objective criteria upon which to base our claim: this man is corrupt (and therefore bad), that man is honest (and therefore good).

For Jesus, the issue was more complicated. He criticised all forms of wrongdoing, but never assigned a single person to the good or bad category. Jesus knew how people often promised one thing and then failed to do it. He recognised that even the best people could do wrong, while even the worst could turn away from sin and be reconciled with God. In the mind of Jesus, the only true category for anybody is the category of human being in need of God's grace.

> He came to what was his own, and his own people did not accept him. But to all who received him, who believed in his name, he gave power to become children of God, who were born, not of blood or of the will of the flesh or of the will of man, but of God. (John 1:11-13)

> Ministries should be exercised in a spirit of fraternal service and dedication to the Church, in the name of the Lord. (CCC 2039)

When he went up for election as a student representative in UCD in 1963, I remember voting for him. He was a very articulate young man, full of energy, bright disposition and clearly at ease with everybody. A few years later I got to know him as a seminarian in the Irish College in Rome. Michael Courtney was ordained priest for Clonfert, but later on he joined the Vatican diplomatic service and represented the Pope in many different nations. While making peace in Burundi, he was shot dead by unknown attackers.

Isn't it ironic? It's usually when bad things happen to them that men such as Michael Courtney make the news. Little of their positive work for human wellbeing is noticed – good news is hard to tell. This puts a powerful obligation on everybody committed to following Jesus Christ: unless we tell the good stories, they will not be publicly celebrated and may even be forgotten. Generosity in the service of mankind deserves better.

> We have gifts that differ according to the grace given to us: prophecy, in proportion to faith; ministry, in ministering; the teacher, in teaching; the exhorter, in exhortation; the giver, in generosity; the leader, in diligence; the compassionate, in cheerfulness. (Romans 12:6-8)

> By living with the mind of Christ, Christians hasten the coming of the reign of God, 'a kingdom of justice, love and peace'. (CCC 2046)

Dr Naim Ateek, an Arab Christian, spoke to the staff and students of our Institute. He told us of the day fifty-five years ago when his family was forced from their home by the Israeli army and, along with thousands of other Palestinians, they became refugees in their own land. He described the ongoing occupation by Israel of Palestinian territory, and the economic disaster that has flowed from this and given rise to regular bloody uprisings and a deadly flow of emigration.

How ought the Christian respond to attack? Ateek is adamant: only the way of non-violence is possible for followers of Jesus Christ. His work in the Sabeel Centre tries to bring all Christians closer together in their commitment to peace, but it also connects with Jews and Muslims who have a similar desire for peace. At present, their common witness has little public acceptance and no political endorsement. He asks, will there be any Christians left in the Holy Land?

> For the kingdom of God is not food and drink but righteousness and peace and joy in the Holy Spirit. (Romans 14:17)

> The 'ten words' point out the conditions of a life freed from the slavery of sin. The Decalogue is a path of life. (CCC 2057)

The students were surprised to learn that the Ten Commandments are also known as the 'Ten Words'. Anybody who hears talk of 'commandments' tends to think primarily about rules, guilt, sin and the ruthless will of a despot or dictator. No Jewish person would think of God in these terms. For Jews, God was the creator who gave life and called his people into a loving covenant. When God spoke a 'word' this meant light in darkness and liberation from captivity.

Calling the Ten Commandments by its older title, 'Ten Words', encourages us to think of morality in terms of life and creativity. It challenges people of faith to live morally, not to avoid punishment, but to discover the life-giving power of love. The 'Ten Words' of Jewish tradition, treasured equally by Christians, describe a world where the values of truth and compassion give light and freedom to a dark and punishing world.

> If you obey the commandments of the LORD your God that I am commanding you today, by loving the LORD your God, walking in his ways, and observing his commandments, decrees, and ordinances, then you shall live and become numerous, and the LORD your God will bless you in the land that you are entering to possess. But if your heart turns away and you do not hear, but are led astray to bow down to other gods and serve them, I declare to you today that you shall perish; you shall not live long in the land that you are crossing the Jordan to enter and possess. (Deuteronomy 30:16-18)

> The Ten Commandments state what is required in the love of God and love of neighbour. The first three concern love of God, and the other seven love of neighbour. (CCC 2067)

Six years ago in the Mater Dei Institute, we witnessed an historical event. Then Taoiseach, Bertie Ahern, and all the major Irish religious leaders came to celebrate the launch of our IT services, including our in-career education for teachers of religion and a live video conferencing link with Belfast. The speeches referred to ecumenism, inter-religious dialogue, north-south contacts and the ongoing educational efforts to enrich knowledge and information with wisdom and understanding.

This is a critical time for religion. Many religious people have claimed religious sanction for acts of terror, and many atheists have accused religion of being anti-life. How can religious faith encourage murder on the one hand, and generate love and compassion on the other? For centuries each great world religion has had to face these questions and find answers from within its own faith. Now is surely the time to face such questions together.

> For whoever keeps the whole law but fails in one point has become accountable for all of it. For the one who said, 'You shall not commit adultery', also said, 'You shall not murder'. Now if you do not commit adultery but if you murder, you have become a transgressor of the law. (James 2:10-11)

> The Ten Commandments belong to God's revelation. At the same time they teach us the true humanity of man. (CCC 2070)

A single actor recounting the life and recalling the works of Charles Dickens – that night in the Gaiety was a magical performance. We were captivated, enraptured and energised. We were invited to enter into the imagination of Dickens and see how a great city can be evoked in fiction. We were helped to feel his critique of Victorian standards and join with him in the celebration of normal living and ordinary people.

Dickens seems to have been a driven man: his marriage was explosive, and many people close to him suffered from the fall-out. But his vision still retains its vitality. Anything humanly demeaning is challenged, while anything humanly enriching is encouraged. His literary output had a strong prophetic quality, building up the good in people and tearing down the bad. He may have been far from perfect, but his work helps us today to aspire to a better world for all.

> This is my commandment, that you love one another as I have loved you. No one has greater love than this, to lay down one's life for one's friends. You are my friends if you do what I command you. (John 15:12-14)

'You shall love the Lord your God with all your heart, and with all your soul, and with all your mind'

> The worship of the one God sets man free from turning in on himself, from the slavery of sin and the idolatry of the world. (CCC 2097)

We were on summer holidays in the Mediterranean island of Malta. One afternoon, there was a minor interruption in the weather. Instead of the usual and predictable clear blue sky and baking sun, some totally unexpected grey clouds arrived from the west and covered the sky in a few moments. I could almost imagine I was home in Ireland, except it was still far too hot. But the clouds brought much relief and the prospect of some serious walking.

The next day was partly clouded, so I took the opportunity to visit the megalithic temples in the south of the island. The people who built these monuments were as sophisticated as any Egyptian pyramid builder or any Irish burial-chamber architect. What prompted these ancestors of ours to build such impressive stone buildings?

> And Mary said, 'My soul magnifies the Lord, and my spirit rejoices in God my Saviour, for he has looked with favour on the lowliness of his servant. Surely, from now on all generations will call me blessed; for the Mighty One has done great things for me, and holy is his name. (Luke 1:46-49)

Idolatry consists in divinising what is not God.
(CCC 2113)

Iran played Ireland in the first leg of a critical qualifying
match for the 2002 World Cup. Thousands of Iranians
were in Dublin. I thought about days of yore when the
Persian Empire straddled most of the near east, when its
armies laid waste the Greek city-states and scattered
even the powerful Roman legions. Today the Empire is
gone, but a proud people remain, languishing under a
very strict Islamic Constitution. Football focuses hope
and celebration.

When the faithful Irish supporters travelled for the
return match to Tehran, they found there a very dry city;
but this return game was played in as sporting an
atmosphere as the one in Dublin. One famous soccer
coach said about football, 'It's not simply a matter of life
and death, it's more important'. National pride, gifted
players and exciting contests are very important realities,
but do they really amount to that?

Be sure of this, that no fornicator or impure
person, or one who is greedy (that is, an idolater),
has any inheritance in the kingdom of Christ and
of God. (Ephesians 5:5)

> Atheism is often based on a false conception of human autonomy, exaggerated to the point of refusing any dependence on God. (CCC 2126)

It was an ordinary classroom full of teenage girls, in a Catholic school in Dublin. Religion class progressed according to plan with an effort to translate the Beatitudes into guidelines for living today. Then one girl put her hand up, called the teacher over and said: 'Miss, I don't believe in God'. The teacher's reaction was interesting. She took the comment at face value, assigned some other (non-Religious) work to the girl and continued with the lesson.

During the often traumatic teen years, it is not unusual to declare one's atheism. For some, it may be a first assertion of personal autonomy: 'I am now my own person and so I refuse to accept what older people have told me'. As the pupil gets older and establishes a firm sense of identity, this lapse into atheism may well prove to be temporary. However, the pupil may genuinely not believe in God, and may only have discovered this fact for the first time. Religion teachers meet both kinds of atheism and need to distinguish well between them.

> I am grateful to Christ Jesus our Lord, who has strengthened me, because he judged me faithful and appointed me to his service, even though I was formerly a blasphemer, a persecutor, and a man of violence. But I received mercy because I had acted ignorantly in unbelief, and the grace of our Lord overflowed for me with the faith and love that are in Christ Jesus. (1 Timothy 1:12-14)

[God] is 'the author of beauty' (Wisdom 13:3).
(CCC 2129)

Pushing my mother in a wheelchair around the grounds of the hospice is a pleasant task in the fine weather. The wind affects her, so she needs her fleece jackets and dressing gowns. She says little, but occasionally indicates with her thumb which way to turn. For weeks she used to point to a lane, which I believed went nowhere, so I never followed that instruction. How wrong I was! Apparently she had gone in there often before and obviously wanted to return.

It was my brother who alerted me to this lane, and to the flower garden in the small hidden courtyard within. On arrival there, one is immediately struck by the variety of flowers, possibly because they are so close to the eye. Every day now I make it my business to bring my mother in there, just to see the effect the flowers have on her. Her condition may leave her confused and unsure, but it hasn't affected her sense of colour and beauty.

> If through delight in the beauty of these things people assumed them to be gods, let them know how much better than these is their Lord, for the author of beauty created them. And if people were amazed at their power and working, let them perceive from them how much more powerful is the one who formed them. For from the greatness and beauty of created things comes a corresponding perception of their Creator. (Wisdom 13:3-5)

> Respect for his name is an expression of the respect owed to the mystery of God himself ... The sense of the sacred is part of the virtue of religion. (CCC 2144)

The story of Atlantis has caught the human imagination for thousands of years. This city, according to Plato, was home to a very sophisticated people and was totally destroyed in a major flood. Some writers, in recent years, have theorised that survivors from Atlantis crossed the seas and brought with them certain elements of their culture, such as pyramids and hieroglyphic writing.

Though few scientists today accept this hypothesis, all remain fascinated by the fact that civilisation appears to have developed simultaneously all over the world, in places as diverse as Egypt, Mesopotamia, China, India and Central America. Interestingly, religious ritual and belief were an integral part of all these great early cultures. What is the future of religion in modern culture?

> Sing to the LORD, bless his name; tell of his salvation from day to day. (Psalms 96:2)

> In Baptism ... the Christian receives his name in the Church. This can be the name of a saint, that is, of a disciple who has lived a life of exemplary fidelity to the Lord. (CCC 2156)

When Pope John Paul II died, there was a brief ceremony to verify his death. The Vatican official called his name three times and, getting no response, pronounced him dead. I was fascinated to realise that the name called out in that Papal Apartment was not any of his major titles, such as Pope or Bishop of Rome or Patriarch of the West. Instead, he was called by his own name given to him by his parents the day he was baptised: Karol Wojtyla.

There is something very special about this little ceremony. Though the world knew the Pope as a great spiritual leader, a powerful voice for justice and peace, a man of dialogue and outreach to others, and a talented writer and linguist, nevertheless, the most basic fact about him is that, like 1.1 billion other Catholics, Karol was baptised into the Body of Christ. His baptismal dignity is ultimately what matters.

> And Jesus came and said to them, 'All authority in heaven and on earth has been given to me. Go therefore and make disciples of all nations, baptising them in the name of the Father and of the Son and of the Holy Spirit, and teaching them to obey everything that I have commanded you. And remember, I am with you always, to the end of the age'. (Matthew 28:18-20)

> God calls each one by name (cf Isaiah 43:1).
> (CCC 2167)

The documentary was about feral children. It listed instances from all over the world of children abandoned by parents and often raised by animals, usually dogs. The efforts people made to reintegrate these children usually involved helping them to learn language and become empathetic. The underlying assumption was obvious: to be a human is to be in touch with other humans, both cognitively and emotionally.

The children found at a young age were better able to make progress; some who were rescued when they had already reached their teens seemed incapable of learning the skills of language. This implies that children need helpful human contact if they are to thrive as people. Equally, one might suggest that if people are to grow spiritually, then they need to hear God speaking their name and declaring his love for them.

> The one who enters by the gate is the shepherd of the sheep. The gatekeeper opens the gate for him, and the sheep hear his voice. He calls his own sheep by name and leads them out. When he has brought out all his own, he goes ahead of them, and the sheep follow him because they know his voice. They will not follow a stranger, but they will run from him because they do not know the voice of strangers. (John 10:2-5)

> The Sunday celebration of the Lord's Day and his Eucharist is at the heart of the Church's life. (CCC 2177)

I dropped in to the Pro-Cathedral at about eleven o'clock one Saturday morning. It was fascinating to observe the crowds of people gathering for Mass. They were under no obligation to be there; they simply wanted to pray together. I guessed that a similar phenomenon was happening in many other churches throughout the land. While the numbers attending church on Sundays has declined, the attendance rate on weekdays has been maintained.

How is one to interpret these facts? Are they a sign that fewer, but more devout people, will make up the congregations of the future? If so, how will contact be kept with those who absent themselves? Will those who come to church, seldom or never, still maintain a life of faith and discipleship? How will Irish life be affected by these changes in religious practice? What will evangelisation look like in Ireland in another generation?

> They devoted themselves to the apostles' teaching and fellowship, to the breaking of bread and the prayers. Awe came upon everyone, because many wonders and signs were being done by the apostles. All who believed were together and had all things in common; they would sell their possessions and goods and distribute the proceeds to all, as any had need. Day by day, as they spent much time together in the temple, they broke bread at home and ate their food with glad and generous hearts, praising God and having the goodwill of all the people. And day by day the Lord added to their number those who were being saved. (Acts 2:42-47)

> You cannot pray at home as at church, where there is a great multitude, where exclamations are cried out to God as from one great heart, and where there is something more: the union of minds, the accord of souls, the bond of charity, the prayer of the priests (St John Chrysostom). (CCC 2179)

I was invited to go to a Christmas show in the National Concert Hall. Gearóid Grant was conducting the RTÉ Concert Orchestra, together with four noted singers, in a medley of festive music. The title of the concert hinted that there would be a chance for everybody to sing along from time to time. It was a great evening's entertainment, in which one heard all the usual carols and seasonal fare. The words of the songs were screened up high for those who needed help with the lyrics.

My reflection soon focussed on the conductor. He did a superb job, coordinating the various musicians, all the singers and the willing audience. His contribution was critical: the entire evening flowed smoothly and enjoyably. Without his supportive role, none of the myriad talents present could have shone forth. Here, perhaps, is an image of the pastor among his faithful people, coaxing them into creative and productive activity and giving them a chance to live life to the full.

> When you come together, it is not really to eat the Lord's supper. For when the time comes to eat, each of you goes ahead with your own supper, and one goes hungry and another becomes drunk. (1 Corinthians 11:20-21)

> The precept of the Church specifies the law of the Lord more precisely: 'On Sundays and other holy days of obligation the faithful are bound to participate in the Mass'. (CCC 2180)

The Church has always been made up of people who worship often and those who go less frequently. In the Middle Ages, matters became so bad, and so few people were attending Mass, that Rome introduced a law obliging Catholics to attend Mass on all Sundays and Holy Days. This was generally interpreted as a serious law, the breaking of which could be grounds for mortal sin. The practice of poor attendance, however, still continued in many lands.

Poor attenders are often called 'non-practising Catholics', and many pastoral strategies have been developed to encourage them to come back and worship. Now they are referred to as 'submarine Catholics'. Most of the time they are invisible, but they surface occasionally at Christmas or Easter, for weddings or funerals, at Christenings and First Communions. How should the sailors, rowing the barque of Peter through stormy waters, greet these absent friends?

> Observe the sabbath day and keep it holy, as the LORD your God commanded you. Six days you shall labour and do all your work. But the seventh day is a sabbath to the LORD your God; you shall not do any work – you, or your son or your daughter, or your male or female slave, or your ox or your donkey, or any of your livestock, or the resident alien in your towns, so that your male and female slave may rest as well as you. (Deuteronomy 5:12-14)

> The institution of Sunday helps all 'to be allowed sufficient rest and leisure to cultivate their familial, cultural, social and religious lives'
> (Gaudium et spes, 67#3). (CCC 2194)

We were near Manor Kilbride in Co. Wicklow on Sunday afternoon. The beaglers were running through the fields, jumping over drains and climbing under wire fences as the hounds moved ahead in search of a scent. Paul was in the lead and he brought us into a pretty, level field, almost surrounded by the infant Liffey. It could easily have been called Liffey Valley. Thoughts of another place of the same name came to our minds, and we were glad to be here rather than there.

Sunday used to be a day of prayer and relaxation. Morning would mean Mass, and after family lunch we would go to public parks to walk and feed the ducks. Now, for many mobile people, Sunday has become a time of hassle, pressure and serious shopping. Are we better off than our parents because we can do all the weekly shopping on Sunday? Do we not all need moments of peace and silence to stay in touch with our deepest selves, where God might want to speak?

> Six days shall work be done, but the seventh day is a sabbath of solemn rest, holy to the LORD. (Exodus 31:15)

'You shall love your neighbour as yourself'

> God has willed that, after him, we should honour our
> parents to whom we owe life and who have handed on
> to us the knowledge of God. (CCC 2197)

At his funeral Mass, Nedser was lamented by a very
large number of relatives, even including some great
grandchildren. Since his wife died some seven years
earlier, he had never been the same. The many tragedies
that befell his extended family during those years and the
deterioration of his own health were a patchwork of
suffering, to which his own sad death, on the first day of
his holidays, was cruelly stitched on by the rough hand
of fate.

Why do some families seem to suffer so much? Is there
any fairness in the way tragedy strikes good-living
people? These questions were in the hearts of many who
gathered in prayer at Mass. Nedser's eldest son spoke
movingly about the simple goodness he had known in his
father, and advised all present to let no time pass before
they spoke to their fathers these powerful words, 'I love
you, Da'.

> Children, obey your parents in the Lord, for this is
> right. 'Honour your father and mother' – this is the
> first commandment with a promise: 'so that it
> may be well with you and you may live long on
> the earth'. (Ephesians 6:1-3)

> The family must be helped and defended by appropriate social measures. Where families cannot fulfil their responsibilities, other social bodies have the duty of helping them and of supporting the institution of the family. (CCC 2209)

When people are ill, they go to the doctor or to hospital and receive the care they require. At least, that is the way we often imagine life to be. However, there are many people who have chronic complaints and the burden of caring for them falls primarily on their parents, who must attend to them at home. A recent TV programme highlighted the stresses often associated with looking after children who have certain intellectual disabilities – in this case, the children all suffered various forms of autism.

The image of a frustrated young teenager, beating his head against the bedroom wall, was very disturbing. The face of a sleep-deprived father, calming a few of his crying children in the middle of the night, was deeply upsetting and confusing. Where is the medical and educational assistance that should be provided for these children? Where is the support for their mothers, fathers and siblings? As a nation, do we treat these children as if they were truly our brothers and sisters, and so our common responsibility?

> If any of your kin fall into difficulty and become dependent on you, you shall support them; they shall live with you as though resident aliens. (Leviticus 25:35)

> The fourth commandment reminds grown children of their responsibilities toward their parents. As much as they can, they must give them material and moral support in old age and in times of illness, loneliness or distress. (CCC 2218)

The number of elderly people in Europe is growing each year, while the percentage of young people is getting smaller. This means that the demands on services for the elderly or infirm will be increasing at just the same time as the ability to pay for these services will be lessening, because fewer (young) people will be paying taxes. Will all old people have to move to nursing homes before they die? Will it be possible to care for them in their own homes?

The Jewish tradition has a commandment, 'Honour your father and mother'. This has often been interpreted, within the Christian tradition, as a call upon children to obey their parents. But surely its scope is greater than that? Surely this commandment, this word from God, is a challenge to adult children to look after their parents when they are old and sick and in need of attentive care?

> The glory of one's father is one's own glory, and it is a disgrace for children not to respect their mother. My child, help your father in his old age, and do not grieve him as long as he lives; even if his mind fails, be patient with him; because you have all your faculties do not despise him. (Sirach 3:11-13)

> Parents have the first responsibility for the education of their children. They bear witness to this responsibility first by creating a home where tenderness, forgiveness, respect, fidelity and disinterested service are the rule. (CCC 2223)

It is customary, in educational writing, for the author to admit that education is wider than what happens in schools. However, most educational writings deal almost exclusively with the form of education offered to children and young people in schools. When an attempt is made to broaden the field, authors write about 'adult education', 'continuing education' or 'community education'.

A recent book by Finola Cunnane, *New Directions in Religious Education*, seriously considers the insight that education is truly life-long and happens in places other than school or community centres. Drawing inspiration from Gabriel Moran, she outlines the four major educational forms: family, schooling, job and leisure/retirement. She then explores the opportunities for religious education in family, school and parish. This is a very insightful and practical book, deserving of a careful read.

> And, fathers, do not provoke your children to anger, but bring them up in the discipline and instruction of the Lord. (Ephesians 6:4)

> It is the duty of citizens to contribute along with the civil authorities to the good of society in a spirit of truth, justice, solidarity and freedom. (CCC 2239)

There was a time when we prized education in Ireland, but the poor state of many of our primary schools makes one doubt the sincerity of our claims to cherish all the children of our nation equally. Then we saw images of the pre-fabricated classroom in Co. Limerick where a large section of the roof fell onto the floor during the day. Luckily, no children were seriously injured. There is no money available, we are told, to do any more than simply repair the roof.

Meanwhile, the names of nearly three hundred tax defaulters were published. People from every walk of life were listed there. Many had bogus offshore accounts; all had failed to pay their fair share of the national tax burden. Where has decency gone? Where has honesty gone? Where has patriotism gone? Where has solidarity gone? These used to be great Irish qualities.

> For the same reason you also pay taxes, for the authorities are God's servants, busy with this very thing. Pay to all what is due them – taxes to whom taxes are due, revenue to whom revenue is due, respect to whom respect is due, honour to whom honour is due. (Romans 13:6-7)

> The fifth commandment forbids direct and intentional killing as gravely sinful. (CCC 2268)

A man's body was found in a large suitcase in the Royal Canal near Croke Park. He had obviously been murdered. What a way to die. Who is he, who are his parents and who are his brothers and sisters? Why did another human being kill him? What wrong was he punished for? What has happened to society that killings such as this are now so common?

Human life is the greatest gift of God. Each human being, even our enemy, even the one we hate, is made in the image and likeness of God. To kill another human being is a terrible sin and a serious crime. Murder is an affront to humanity. There must be some better way of settling our differences than simply eliminating them.

> You have heard that it was said to those of ancient times, 'You shall not murder'; and 'whoever murders shall be liable to judgement.' But I say to you that if you are angry with a brother or sister, you will be liable to judgement; and if you insult a brother or sister, you will be liable to the council; and if you say, 'You fool,' you will be liable to the hell of fire. (Matthew 5:21-22)

> Those whose lives are diminished or weakened deserve special respect. Sick or handicapped persons should be helped to lead lives as normal as possible. (CCC 2276)

The news was shocking: it concerned the remains of an elderly man being exhumed from a grave in Baltinglass for an autopsy, because fears had been expressed about the nature of his death. A nurse who cared for him in hospital had just been fired, allegedly because of suspicion that she had given him and some other patients more drugs than they needed. Could this be a case of murder or manslaughter?

The family of the elderly man had no suspicion that anything was amiss. They, like most people, trusted the hospital and its staff. Without trust no real life is possible. However, sometimes our trust is betrayed, and those we depend on turn out to be unreliable. Ireland knows all too well of church people who were abusive, and of politicians and business folk who scorned the law. Who cares for the carers? Who guards the guardians?

> After leaving the synagogue he entered Simon's house. Now Simon's mother-in-law was suffering from a high fever, and they asked him about her. Then he stood over her and rebuked the fever, and it left her. Immediately she got up and began to serve them. As the sun was setting, all those who had any who were sick with various kinds of diseases brought them to him; and he laid his hands on each of them and cured them. (Luke 4:38-40)

> Suicide contradicts the natural inclination of the human being to preserve and perpetuate his life. (CCC 2281)

When people die in road accidents, the facts are published in all the newspapers and on TV. It is well we are reminded of these tragedies, because they are a cancer at the heart of Irish society. And yet, in any given year, there are more people who commit suicide than are killed on the road. This is especially true of young adolescent men. For some reason, we are loath to face this harsh reality. Do we feel a certain responsibility for the disaster?

What is causing the young to take their own lives? Is the issue a medical one: are the young people depressed and unable to live? Is the issue one of personal development: are some males so unsure about their sexual orientation that they abscond from the challenge? Is the issue a social one: what impossible expectations are placed on them, so that they buckle under the pressure? More importantly, what can the older population do to minimise the trauma?

> 'Teacher, which commandment in the law is the greatest?' He said to him, 'You shall love the Lord your God with all your heart, and with all your soul, and with all your mind.' This is the greatest and first commandment. And a second is like it: 'You shall love your neighbour as yourself'. (Matthew 22:36-39)

> Terrorism threatens, wounds and kills indiscriminately; it is gravely against justice and charity. (CCC 2297)

When bombs are dropped and innocent civilians are killed, it is called 'collateral damage'. We are told that such mistakes occur because the 'intelligence community' has not yet penetrated the heart of the terrorists. War is indeed a strange phenomenon. It allows language to be twisted as often as buildings and human bodies. No dead father is lamented for being 'collateral damage'. Spies do not write 'intelligence community' on their passports.

If language, designed for communication, becomes dense and confusing, then war has truly been victorious – for it has succeeded in killing the Word. We believe that the Word was God in the beginning, and that the Word was made flesh for our salvation. Word, at best, has life-giving power. Human word reflects divine Word; twist the human word, and you twist the creative power of humans. How can we fight against such distortion? Is there a just war against the abuse of language?

> Their infants will be dashed to pieces before their eyes; their houses will be plundered, and their wives ravished. See, I am stirring up the Medes against them, who have no regard for silver and do not delight in gold. Their bows will slaughter the young men; they will have no mercy on the fruit of the womb; their eyes will not pity children. (Isaiah 13:16-18)

> Peace cannot be attained on earth without safeguarding
> the goods of persons, free communication among men,
> respect for the dignity of persons and peoples, and the
> assiduous practice of fraternity. (CCC 2304)

Assisi remains a beautiful city in spite of the earthquake
eight years ago. The damage to the Basilica of St Francis
has been repaired. The tourists and pilgrims crowd the
streets and visit the tombs of Francis and Clare. Life goes
on as normal – but then one notices the cranes. Unlike
Dublin, where they speak of economic growth, here the
cranes speak of homelessness. Though the artwork and
architecture has long since been repaired, the houses of
ordinary people still remain at risk and hundreds of local
people are still living in prefabs.

It is like the problem in the Holy Land. Everybody wants
to visit the buildings associated with Jesus, but few
recognise the 'living stones', the people who believe in
him and live in his land. Francis and Clare preached a
Gospel of peace. This peace has a Hebrew name: *shalom*.
Peace implies the absence of war, but it goes well beyond
this to include all forms of human wellbeing. The peace
of God means fullness of life. As long as houses are
unavailable to the people, the peace of God has not
returned to Assisi.

> You have heard that it was said, 'You shall love your
> neighbour and hate your enemy.' But I say to you,
> Love your enemies and pray for those who persecute
> you, so that you may be children of your Father in
> heaven; for he makes his sun rise on the evil and
> on the good, and sends rain on the righteous and on
> the unrighteous. (Matthew 5:43-45)

> Because of the evils and injustices that all war brings with it, we must do everything reasonably possible to avoid it. (CCC 2327)

The IRA was very, very slow to decommission its weapons. Now that its arms are verifiably out of use, most people are overjoyed and can sense that progress is being made, and that a certain Rubicon has been crossed. Is the war finally over? What other blind alleyways must we enter before the clear vistas of peace are revealed? And, in particular, what about Loyalist arms and violence?

If it takes two to tango, it often takes more than two to make peace. Our hope and our prayer each day must be for all violence to stop, no matter from what source it comes – the injured and the dead don't really care whether their pain was due to Republican violence, Loyalist atrocities or State terrorism. Loyalty to one's roots can surely be integrated into loyalty to the State. The State should be something that nourishes the entire public, and to which all can belong with conviction.

> Blessed are the peacemakers, for they will be called children of God. (Matthew 5:9)

> In creating men 'male and female', God gives man and woman an equal personal dignity (Familiaris Consortio, 22). (CCC 2334)

Religion and Gender, by Sandra Cullen (published by Veritas), is a commentary on one of the optional sections in the Leaving Certificate Religious Education syllabus. It examines in great detail how each of the world's major religions treat men and women. Historically, men have 'called the shots' in religion. However, careful reading of many sacred texts allows us today to highlight the place of women in religious life and discourse.

In terms of Judaism, as well as talking about Joseph and David, the author introduces us to Deborah and Miriam, two powerful prophetic women. In the context of Christianity, Jesus' dealings with the Syro-Phoenician woman and Mary Magdalen are highlighted in order to show what Christians have lost by forgetting how radical was the stance of their Master. Hildegard of Bingen and Dorothy Day are treated in terms of their powerful impact on issues of spirituality and justice.

> This is the list of the descendants of Adam. When God created humankind, he made them in the likeness of God. Male and female he created them, and he blessed them and named them 'Humankind' when they were created. (Genesis 5:1-2)

> Prostitution does injury to the dignity of the person who engages in it, reducing the person to an instrument of sexual pleasure ... Prostitution is a social scourge. (CCC 2355)

According to all reputable history books, slavery has been abolished throughout the world. No religious philosophy tries to justify it, and no secular ideology would condone it. No country admits to having any slaves, and yet the reality is very different. Millions of women and young children in India are forced to work in the clothing and construction industries for such a pittance that they are slaves in all but name.

Even Ireland has its slaves – they are often from outside the European Union, and come to find employment in our wealthy economy. They become lap dancers or prostitutes before they realise what's taking place. They are forced to do degrading work in what is loosely called 'the sex industry'. They are not technically slaves, but their lifestyle is inhuman, their bosses regularly abuse them and they are often without hope for the future. This is modern-day slavery.

> Do you not know that your bodies are members of Christ? Should I therefore take the members of Christ and make them members of a prostitute? Never! Do you not know that whoever is united to a prostitute becomes one body with her? For it is said, 'The two shall be one flesh'. (1 Corinthians 6:15-16)

> Sexuality is ordered to the conjugal love of man and woman. (CCC 2360)

I hadn't been talking to her for quite some time, but I recognised her voice on the phone: 'I hope you can make it next Saturday evening; we're having a party to celebrate our twenty-fifth wedding anniversary'. The fact that a quarter of a century had passed since that day was very hard to grasp. Can time pass so quickly? Then the memories emerged: arranging the date in early 1979, and then, later on, discovering that the Pope was coming to Ireland on the very same day.

The wedding was booked for the church in Swords, the parish of Dublin Airport. As this was where the Pope was due to land, I had to spend the night before the wedding near the church, because the streets were blocked for security reasons. I recall eating my breakfast as the plane circled the Phoenix Park and watching the ceremonies on TV. It was a memorable wedding on a historical day.

> So she got up, and they began to pray and implore that they might be kept safe. Tobias began by saying, 'Blessed are you, O God of our ancestors, and blessed is your name in all generations forever. Let the heavens and the whole creation bless you forever. You made Adam, and for him you made his wife Eve as a helper and support. From the two of them the human race has sprung. You said, "It is not good that the man should be alone; let us make a helper for him like himself." I now am taking this kinswoman of mine, not because of lust, but with sincerity. Grant that she and I may find mercy and that we may grow old together.' And they both said, 'Amen, Amen.' Then they went to sleep for the night. (Tobit 8:5-9)

> Connected to incest is any sexual abuse perpetrated by adults on children or adolescents entrusted to their care. (CCC 2389)

Maria Goretti was repeatedly stabbed by a man trying to rape her, and she died at the age of twelve in 1902. When Pope Pius XII canonised her, he said: 'Not all of us are called to undergo martyrdom, but we are all called to a life of Christian virtue. Now virtue demands courage. It may not reach the heights attained by this young girl. Nevertheless, it demands from us daily, assiduous, unremitting effort to our very last breath, and so it can be called a slow and continuous martyrdom'.

Since then we have come to learn much more about the sexual abuse of children. Studies have explained some of the reasons why it happens, and also the very serious long-term effects it can have on the abused. We have also, to our horror, learned that this abuse is widespread in society and happens within families, schools, youth clubs and parish houses. The guilty need to be apprehended and punished for their crime and given treatment for their illness.

> But Absalom spoke to Amnon neither good nor bad; for Absalom hated Amnon, because he had raped his sister Tamar. (2 Samuel 13:22)

> Chastity means the integration of sexuality within the person. It includes an apprenticeship in self-mastery. (CCC 2395)

In the Christian vision of life, sexuality is a powerful gift from a creative and life-bestowing God, given to all God's creatures so that they can flourish in their full humanity as bodily and relational beings. God is love and humans are made in God's image, therefore love is the greatest human value. The moral challenge confronting sexual beings is to integrate sexuality into this movement of creative love.

Many elements of modern culture make it hard for people to achieve this integration – an obvious example is the pressure experienced in the workplace. More serious is the expansion of internet pornography. But now there is a new hurdle to jump: images of smiling female faces invite us to dial a number and let the flirting begin. There is nothing very wrong in that, you might think. But is this kind of contact not a flight from reality, rather than a generous embrace of real sexual love?

> Likewise, urge the younger men to be self-controlled. (Titus 2:6)

> Even if it does not contradict the provision of civil law, any form of unjustly taking and keeping the property of others is against the seventh commandment: thus, deliberate retention of goods lent or of objects lost; business fraud; paying unjust wages; forcing up prices by taking advantage of the ignorance or hardship of another. (CCC 2409)

A number of years ago, the Thai authorities discovered a major business scam. Relying on the sophistication of the Thai phone system, an international company promised high returns and encouraged people to buy shares in what turned out to be non-existent companies. Many of the purchasers lived in Australia and New Zealand. Many of the fraudsters were Irish and the alleged brain of the operation was an Irishman.

The world of today gives new opportunities for dishonesty. Stealing from shops and houses still continues, but far more subtle ways of stealing now exist. Computer crime, white-collar crime and fraud on a global scale – these are the new forms of stealing, but they remain as wrong as any of their earlier forms. In some respects, they may even be worse. For often the stealing/thieving/fraud is committed by well-educated, sophisticated people who have no need to acquire more funds. It used to be said that Ireland was not so much 'the land of saints and scholars', but rather an Ireland of 'rogues and robbers'. Are we simply living up to our reputation?

> Hear this, you that trample on the needy, and bring to ruin the poor of the land, saying, 'When will the new moon be over so that we may sell grain; and the sabbath, so that we may offer wheat for sale? We will make the ephah small and the shekel great, and practice deceit with false balances, buying the poor for silver and the needy for a pair of sandals, and selling the sweepings of the wheat'. (Amos 8:4-6)

> The seventh commandment enjoins respect for the integrity of creation. (CCC 2415)

Weather extremes have been noted all over the world. High temperatures and raging bushfires in one area have been matched by flooding and hurricane winds in others. The Greenland ice-cap has shrunk considerably and scientists fear that the ice around the North Pole will soon be all gone. The Chinese are seeding the clouds and trying to produce rainfall in the Tibetan highlands.

Questions are being asked about possible major changes in the climate of the world. Some suggest that human activity is contributing substantially to the heating of the atmosphere, which brings flooding to many parts and leaves other regions deprived of water altogether. The confidence of humans in their own ability to organise the world the way they wish is growing less each day.

> God blessed them, and God said to them, 'Be fruitful and multiply, and fill the earth and subdue it; and have dominion over the fish of the sea and over the birds of the air and over every living thing that moves upon the earth.' God said, 'See, I have given you every plant yielding seed that is upon the face of all the earth, and every tree with seed in its fruit; you shall have them for food. And to every beast of the earth, and to every bird of the air, and to everything that creeps on the earth, everything that has the breath of life, I have given every green plant for food.' And it was so. God saw everything that he had made, and indeed, it was very good. (Genesis 1:28-31)

> The Church makes a moral judgement about economic and social matters, 'when the fundamental rights of the person or the salvation of souls requires it' (Gaudium et spes, 76#5). (CCC 2420)

When Karl Marx evaluated the state of religion in Europe during the nineteenth century, he judged religion to be very remiss in regard to issues of justice and human rights. He claimed that religion was like opium for the believers, drugging their senses to such a degree that they failed to notice the extent of injustice in the world, while they longed passionately for a better life after death.

John Murray's timely book, entitled *Issues of Justice and Peace*, offers Leaving Certificate students a powerful analysis of modern society, while looking in detail at world hunger, poverty and discrimination in Ireland, just war theory and the care of the earth. More importantly, he shows how all the great world religions contribute to the debate about these life-and-death issues. Marx might be surprised at how religion has changed.

> 'No slave can serve two masters; for a slave will either hate the one and love the other, or be devoted to the one and despise the other. You cannot serve God and wealth.' The Pharisees, who were lovers of money, heard all this, and they ridiculed him. (Luke 16:13)

> *Access to employment* and to professions must be
> open to all without unjust discrimination: men
> and women, healthy and disabled *[sic]*, natives
> and immigrants. (CCC 2433)

When Dublin hosted the Special Olympics in 2003, it
was also the European Year of People with Disabilities.
We were all challenged to notice a very subtle change of
language. We often, unthinkingly, used to refer to people
as 'The Blind' or 'The Disabled', as if the crucial issue
was their illness or their condition. Talking this way can
lead us to marginalise these people or to imagine that
they need to be treated very differently to everybody else.

Yet, if we talk about 'people with disability', we are
putting the emphasis where we ought – on their being
'people' just like everybody else, on their common
humanity, which they share with all. Once we get used to
thinking about 'people', then we can also imagine their
dignity, their rights, their gifts, their responsibilities,
their contributions and their beauty. This is a much
healthier way of thinking about our brothers and sisters
who differ slightly from us, while we have practically all
else in common.

> You shall not withhold the wages of poor and needy
> labourers, whether other Israelites or aliens who
> reside in your land in one of your towns. You shall
> pay them their wages daily before sunset, because
> they are poor and their livelihood depends on them;
> otherwise they might cry to the LORD against you,
> and you would incur guilt. (Deuteronomy 24:14-15)

> The goods of creation are destined for the entire human race. The right to private property does not abolish the universal destination of goods. (CCC 2452)

After the tsunami struck in Southeast Asia on St Stephen's day, the dead bodies had to be found and buried quickly. After that, the main challenge was to help the survivors. Above all else, they needed food, water, medicine, clothes and shelter – but it was very difficult to move these items to the remotest areas. Many individual people gave generous donations to international charities. Along with the monies promised by numerous governments, these could purchase much needed relief supplies.

During the traumatic tsunami week, the stories that touched me most were those concerning some Thai people, who though shattered by the events and grieving for their own lost family members, still found time and energy to feed and house some stranded tourists. The human heart is a true wonder: out of nothing can often flow real wealth; out of poverty can emerge riches that last forever. It seems that disaster can teach us how we are all part of one human family.

> Give liberally and be ungrudging when you do so, for on this account the LORD your God will bless you in all your work and in all that you undertake. Since there will never cease to be some in need on the earth, I therefore command you, 'Open your hand to the poor and needy neighbour in your land.' (Deuteronomy 15:10-11)

> The eighth commandment forbids misrepresenting the truth in our relations with others. (CCC 2464)

In March 2002, David Trimble made the international news for some disparaging comments he had made about the Republic of Ireland. If we are truly as bad as he alleges, then he was right to tell us so, as part of ongoing reconciliation between the two traditions in Ireland. The truth is guaranteed to set us all free. But if he exaggerated, if he was not telling the truth, then how can peace prosper in Ireland?

Sticks and stones may break my bones, but words will never hurt me. This item of traditional 'wisdom' is highly suspect. Words are full of power, both to build up and to tear down, both to encourage and to infuriate, both to heal and to torture. As a lawyer, Trimble must have known this fact better than most. He makes a living from the careful crafting of words. Hopefully his next word will be a living word.

> Hear, for I will speak noble things, and from my lips will come what is right; for my mouth will utter truth; wickedness is an abomination to my lips. All the words of my mouth are righteous; there is nothing twisted or crooked in them. (Proverbs 8:6-8)

> Martyrdom is the supreme witness given to the truth of the faith: it means bearing witness even unto death. (CCC 2473)

Murder in the Cathedral is a powerful dramatic tale, which recounts the killing of Thomas Becket by soldiers loyal to King Henry II. The poetry of T.S. Eliot evokes the poverty of the ordinary women of Canterbury, who are 'living and partly living'. The interior drama, wherein four tempters test Becket, reminds one of the temptations of Jesus in the Gospels. The fourth and last temptation is the key one: 'to do the right deed for the wrong reason'.

Was Becket a true martyr, on his own terms, who simply did the will of God as it unfolded in his life, and who neither sought nor avoided the ultimate self-sacrifice? Or was he guilty, as suggested by one of his executioners, of 'suicide while of unsound mind'? The play gives no simple answer. But the English people who, for four centuries, trooped to Canterbury as pilgrims to the tomb of the dead archbishop, gave their own eloquent answer in their own simple way.

> Do not be ashamed, then, of the testimony about our Lord or of me his prisoner, but join with me in suffering for the gospel, relying on the power of God, who saved us and called us with a holy calling, not according to our works but according to his own purpose and grace. (2 Timothy 1:8-9)

> Lying is destructive of society; it undermines trust among men and tears apart the fabric of social relationships. (CCC 2486)

A few years ago, a fifteen-year-old Galway girl reported to the police that she had been abducted and raped in the city by strangers. Though many people have become almost immune to such news, there was a measure of revulsion in the reactions of most. This is entirely understandable; no matter how often rape happens, it still remains an inhuman and destructive crime. People ought to react to it in horror, so that some possible perpetrator may be discouraged.

A week later, we learned that the girl made up the story; it never happened at all. Without wanting to judge her motives for such strange behaviour, it is fair to wonder if this kind of accusation happens very often? Are some people willing to accuse others of crime without reflecting on the possible damage that might accrue to the good name of those accused? Without honesty, society cannot hold. Falsity can destroy not just names but even entire lives.

> It is not right to be partial to the guilty, or to subvert the innocent in judgement. (Proverbs 18:5)

> Etymologically, 'concupiscence' can refer to any intense form of human desire ... It unsettles man's moral faculties and, without being in itself an offence, inclines man to commit sins. (CCC 2515)

We were talking at breakfast to a gentleman who was visiting the Centre in the Seminary at Ushaw near Durham for the day. He had a strong English accent and, as he spoke, Joanne thought he said 'computer sins'. This was a phrase she had never heard before. Wondering what was involved, she asked for clarification. It transpired he was recounting part of a lecture in moral theology in which the topic was 'concupiscence'. We laughed at this strange-sounding word and its confusion with the other.

Later on, though, it struck me that there might be some link between the two. The international trade in internet pornography may have given a new meaning to the notion of 'computer sins'. And, of course, a major contributor to the global problem of pornography is the deeply-rooted inclination to evil that can debase sexual power when one uses the gift of sexuality entirely for self-gratification.

> You have heard that it was said, 'You shall not commit adultery.' But I say to you that everyone who looks at a woman with lust has already committed adultery with her in his heart. (Matthew 5:27)

> The heart is the seat of moral personality: 'Out of the heart come evil thoughts, murder, adultery, fornication ...' (CCC 2517)

When first we heard that a headless man had been found in the Royal Canal, beside our church, we prayed for him at Sunday Mass. Later, his identity was finally revealed: he was a young man from Somalia and had been working in Ireland for eight years. The image of his smiling face greeted us in the papers. How many family did he leave behind? What dream had drawn him here half way around the world?

He was brutally murdered and then dismembered before being dumped in the canal. After excellent detective work, the people responsible for this outrage were eventually brought to trial and sentenced to long terms in prison. They were two young women, and they pleaded that they were defending their mother, who was then living with the man. She has since been charged with his murder.

> For out of the heart come evil intentions, murder, adultery, fornication, theft, false witness, slander. (Matthew 15:19)

> The tenth commandment forbids ... avarice arising from a passion for riches and their attendant power. It also forbids the desire to commit injustice by harming our neighbour in his temporal goods. (CCC 2536)

It was a strange week indeed. My friend Elaine had told us how she was getting petrol when she heard a loud noise; it turned out to be robbers shooting a publican. The evening news reported how these criminals were caught almost as soon as they fled. The following day I drove past where one of them used to live, and I saw a car just outside with all the windows vandalised and the registration plates missing.

Musing on human greed and violence, I was walking on a carpet of beautiful brown leaves. Soon they will be dark, mushy and ugly. They are perhaps a metaphor of human arrogance. The criminal thinks he can beat the system and find happiness in dishonest behaviour. The wealthy man thinks life is good, as long as the funds last and the accounts grow. But all human life is like the leaves: it flourishes for a moment and then fades into dust. May God save us from ourselves and from our foolish passions.

> You shall not covet your neighbour's house; you shall not covet your neighbour's wife, or male or female slave, or ox, or donkey, or anything that belongs to your neighbour. (Exodus 20:17)

> Desire for true happiness frees man from his immoderate attachment to the goods of this world so that he can find his fulfilment in the vision and beatitude of God. (CCC 2548)

It is a small book, but it deals with big issues. It's called *New Life for Old: On Desire and Becoming Human.* The aim of the author, Vincent MacNamara, is to disclose the importance of desire within the project of becoming human. At our deepest core, we are creatures of desire, and if we attend carefully to this dynamic we will not only discover the way to human integration, but find an opening there for the life-giving mystery at the heart of religion, as well as a call to grow as moral beings.

Writing as a Catholic theologian, MacNamara is well aware that our tradition has not always valued the realm of desire; on the contrary, it has often fostered a kind of detachment that would deny desire its proper scope. Against that background, he appeals for a careful attention to the real lives of people as a necessary context for any formulation of religious or moral ideals. Not all people have been graced as favourably as the most gifted, but all are called to human authenticity.

> Do not store up for yourselves treasures on earth, where moth and rust consume and where thieves break in and steal; but store up for yourselves treasures in heaven, where neither moth nor rust consumes and where thieves do not break in and steal. For where your treasure is, there your heart will be also. (Matthew 6:19-21)

> Detachment from riches is necessary for entering the Kingdom of Heaven. 'Blessed are the poor in spirit'. (CCC 2556)

My passenger-side wing mirror was stolen one night, and I noticed its absence the next morning. This was the third time some person (perhaps local?) had taken a mirror off my car. I should have felt happy that the damage wasn't greater. I should have rejoiced that no personal damage had been done – a car is easily fixed. I should have forgiven my enemy and stopped fretting. But 'should' is easier said than done. Ideal finds real very elusive.

So I decided to start praying for my thief. He must be very hard up if he needs three wing mirrors. And I intend to pray also for others who are equally hard up, and therefore tempted to steal property. But my most important prayer will be for myself: may I never feel so attached to anything that losing it robs me of my peace. May I learn to love God more, and love mammon less.

> He called the crowd with his disciples, and said to them, 'If any want to become my followers, let them deny themselves and take up their cross and follow me. For those who want to save their life will lose it, and those who lose their life for my sake, and for the sake of the gospel, will save it'. (Mark 8:34-35)

PART FOUR

Christian Prayer

Introduction

> But when we pray, do we speak from the height of
> our pride and will, or 'out of the depths' of a
> humble and contrite heart? (CCC 2559)

A Jewish Rabbi from London visited the Mater Dei
Institute recently to explore with us the theme of prayer.
He wondered about the practice of praying the cursing
psalms and the psalms of lament. One approach is to
refuse to pray them, and pray only more joyful or
celebratory psalms. But this is to miss something very
central to Jewish spirituality: the sense of a deep
relationship with God, which allows for absolute
honesty from the person of faith.

Though we might want life to be bright and airy, for
many people life is often dark and stressful. When we
come to God in prayer, how could we leave out of our
prayer the darkness of our lives? If we truly feel that God
has been unfair, if we truly find life incomprehensible, if
we are truly wandering in the valley of darkness, then
prayer that neglects these realities is not genuine prayer
at all. *De profundis* (out of the depths) is a good way to
capture the integrity of real prayer.

> The Pharisee, standing by himself, was praying thus,
> 'God, I thank you that I am not like other people:
> thieves, rogues, adulterers, or even like this tax
> collector. I fast twice a week; I give a tenth of all my
> income.' But the tax collector, standing far off, would
> not even look up to heaven, but was beating his breast
> and saying, 'God, be merciful to me, a sinner!' I tell
> you, this man went down to his home justified rather
> than the other; for all who exalt themselves will be
> humbled, but all who humble themselves will
> be exalted. (Luke 18:11-14)

> God calls man first. Man may forget his creator or hide from his face; he may run after idols or accuse the deity of having abandoned him; yet the living and true God tirelessly calls each person to that mysterious encounter known as prayer.
> (CCC 2567)

People today are capable of bowing down before false gods instead of worshipping the true God. Some examples are land, politics, religion, drugs, sex, money or even work. We cannot make an idol out of something evil or rotten or worthless. We can make an idol only out of something that is basically good, valuable, worthwhile, beautiful or attractive. By concentrating on this thing and making it the centre of our life, in such a way that we have no place for God, we worship idols today.

Notice, too, that when we worship these idols, it is not God who suffers but rather human beings. May God the Father of Jesus Christ, the one and only true God, the only God worth worshipping, send down his Holy Spirit to help us recognise all our false gods, all the idols we have created and worshipped, so that recognising them we may turn our backs on them, in order to give our hearts to the one true God.

> From one ancestor he made all nations to inhabit the whole earth, and he allotted the times of their existence and the boundaries of the places where they would live, so that they would search for God and perhaps grope for him and find him – though indeed he is not far from each one of us. (Act 17:26-27)

> The infant Samuel must have learned from his mother Hannah how 'to stand before the Lord' and from the priest Eli how to listen to his word: 'Speak, Lord, for your servant is listening'. (CCC 2578)

A reading at Mass contained the story of Samuel hearing a voice and not knowing who was speaking. Eventually he learns from Eli that it is God who is calling him, speaking to his heart and challenging him to grow in the love of God. The refrain, 'Speak, Lord, your servant is listening', has echoes in the Gospel story as well. There Andrew spends a short time living-in with Jesus, talking to him and listening to him. He decides this is God's anointed one speaking to him, so he invites his brother Simon to come along and hear for himself.

God is a revealing God, therefore God speaks in many different ways. God's voice is often hard to recognise and always hard to respond to. We are not on our own as we try to listen carefully to God's speeches. Others surround us who also have good ears. Others alert us to the rhythms of God's music. This entire project presupposes that we are all like Samuel and Andrew – all able to hear God in the flow of life, but sometimes confused about what God is saying.

> Therefore Eli said to Samuel, 'Go, lie down; and if he calls you, you shall say, "Speak, LORD, for your servant is listening."' So Samuel went and lay down in his place. Now the LORD came and stood there, calling as before, 'Samuel! Samuel!' And Samuel said, 'Speak, for your servant is listening'. (Isaiah 3:9-10)

> Prayed and fulfilled in Christ, the Psalms are an essential and permanent element of the prayer of the Church. They are suitable for men of every condition and time. (CCC 2597)

When Irish traditional music was rediscovered in the 1960s, one composer became a great favourite: the blind harper, Turlough O'Carolan. We came to love his concerto and his planxties. He composed his music for the Irish nobility at a time when savage penal laws tried to eliminate the Gaelic and Catholic culture. But even the poor peasants loved O'Carolan, though his drinking and womanising were legendary.

Brian Keenan, the academic from Belfast who spent over four years as a hostage in Beirut, has written a fine novel called *Turlough*, which reveals O'Carolan's long struggle to give birth to his musical voice in an Ireland under siege. Though O'Carolan was by no means a devout Catholic, he loved the psalms nevertheless. Their cries of hope and frustration, suffering and love, despair and courage echoed in his broken heart. From the cadences of the psalms flowed O'Carolan's beautiful music.

> Do not get drunk with wine, for that is debauchery; but be filled with the Spirit, as you sing psalms and hymns and spiritual songs among yourselves, singing and making melody to the Lord in your hearts, giving thanks to God the Father at all times and for everything in the name of our Lord Jesus Christ. (Ephesians 5:18-20)

> [Jesus] includes all men in his prayer, for he has taken on humanity in his incarnation, and he offers them to the Father when he offers himself. (CCC 2602)

The Israeli Government became so annoyed with the suicide bomb attacks against its citizens that it finally built a wall around the West Bank, in order to control the Arab bombers. There have been infamous walls in the past, especially in Berlin. People also recall the spiritual wall of Apartheid in South Africa. Clearly the Israelis want to separate themselves from their neighbours, and to keep the two nations hermetically sealed from one another.

Thousands of years ago there was a separation wall within the Temple of Jerusalem, which kept Jews and Gentiles apart. It gave outsiders some access to the Temple, but prevented them from meeting and contaminating the religious Jews in this holy location. St Paul, in trying to explain to Jews the meaning of the death and resurrection of Jesus, used the image of breaking down this wall between Jews and Gentiles. Jesus came to unite the separate components of divided humanity.

> For the one who sanctifies and those who are sanctified all have one Father. For this reason Jesus is not ashamed to call them brothers and sisters, saying, 'I will proclaim your name to my brothers and sisters, in the midst of the congregation I will praise you'. (Hebrews 2:11-12)

> Just as Jesus prays to the Father and gives thanks before receiving his gifts, so he teaches us filial boldness: 'Whatever you ask in prayer, believe that you receive it, and you will'. (CCC 2610)

Listening to the story of the frightened disciples in the boat on a stormy night, one quickly thinks of other storms that are rocking the Church today. The clerical sex abuse scandals would have been unthinkable not very long ago, but now they occur with monotonous regularity. They strike suddenly and disruptively, just like the storms that once rolled down from the Golan Heights to threaten the disciples on the Sea of Galilee.

What can save the little boat of Peter? To whom can the terrified occupants turn in their hour of danger? Jesus has already stretched out his hand to rescue Peter, the man of little faith. In grasping that hand with confidence, Peter grew in faith, hope and love. The same Jesus makes the same gesture to all his followers today. It is through catching that outstretched hand (turning to him in prayer) that they can come safely through all life's storms.

> Truly I tell you, if you say to this mountain, 'Be taken up and thrown into the sea,' and if you do not doubt in your heart, but believe that what you say will come to pass, it will be done for you. So I tell you, whatever you ask for in prayer, believe that you have received it, and it will be yours. (Mark 11:23-24)

> Adoration is the first attitude of man acknowledging that he is a creature before his creator. (CCC 2628)

There was some debate about the broadcasting of the Angelus on RTÉ, our national television service. Objections were raised by a few people, arguing either from a secular perspective – that this was brainwashing – or from a religious perspective – that this Catholic practice was objectionable to members of other religious traditions. However, it seems that most of us regard the practice as worth preserving: when we are so busy, so often, we might forget God.

The irony of the Angelus bells on TV was brought home to me recently when I discovered that church bells nowadays in central Dublin seldom ring out the Angelus. The reason given is that people working nearby don't like to be disturbed or reminded of God while they earn their bread. Our parishioners of St Agatha in North William Street voted to restore the Angelus bells and, after a long silence, they now ring out twice a day every day of the week.

> O come, let us sing to the LORD; let us make a joyful noise to the rock of our salvation! Let us come into his presence with thanksgiving; let us make a joyful noise to him with songs of praise! For the LORD is a great God, and a great King above all gods. In his hand are the depths of the earth; the heights of the mountains are his also. The sea is his, for he made it, and the dry land, which his hands have formed. O come, let us worship and bow down, let us kneel before the LORD, our Maker! (Psalms 95:1-6)

Since Abraham, intercession – asking on behalf of another – has been characteristic of a heart attuned to God's mercy. (CCC 2635)

Almost a hundred people were killed at an air show in Ukraine. Nine miners in Pennsylvania, lost for three days in the depths of the earth, were found and restored to their families around the same time. Why all these deaths in one place, and all the rescues in another? Does God have favourites? Was the prayer of the western Americans more powerful than the petition of the eastern Slavs?

One American miner attributed his rescue to God, his wife and his colleagues. The people of Ukraine gathered in church to pray for the dead and especially those still in hospital. America may be a very secular state, and Ukraine may well be suffering the effects of atheistic communism, but when tragedy threatens or strikes, the human response of faith turns many people towards the living God.

Let each of you look not to your own interests, but to the interests of others. (Philippians 2:4)

> As in the prayer of petition, every event and need can become an offering of thanksgiving. (CCC 2638)

We were on summer holidays and rested all day by the pool. It was hot, but a fresh sea breeze kept the air alive. Every so often we took a plunge into the water, or just sat in the shade of the huge yellow umbrellas to read our books. Lunch consisted of a lazy beer and a sandwich in a grotto-like café, where the swallows flew in and out to search for bits of bread, and then swooped to pick them up when nobody was looking.

This was a day of doing absolutely nothing. But it was also a day for noticing little details, such as the man with one leg, seated calmly in his wheelchair, surrounded by wife and family. Was it an accident, we wondered. We learned this was not so, but rather an operation that went wrong. This was a day for giving thanks to God for the small little complaints that keep us talking each day. How fortunate we are to be able to stand up on both legs and get around from place to place!

> Give thanks in all circumstances; for this is the will of God in Christ Jesus for you. (1 Thessalonians 5:18)

> Prayer of praise is entirely disinterested and rises to God, lauds him and gives him glory for his own sake, quite beyond what he has done, but simply because He Is. (CCC 2649)

In a silent world I suddenly heard a bird singing. In the spring sunshine the song was gentle and caressing. The silence largely remained but it was no longer oppressive. Life coursed through the veins of the air, and it felt great to be alive. How can mere bird-song have this powerful effect on the human spirit? Is there more to it than meets the eye or greets the ear? Is bird-song a gift of God?

I recalled a phrase by Tertullian, the father of Latin theology. Writing to pagans in North Africa eighteen hundred years ago, he said: 'The whole creation prays ... the birds taking flight lift themselves up to heaven and instead of hands spread out the cross of their wings, while saying something which may be supposed to be a prayer'. If all creation comes from God the Father through His Word, then the prayer of the Word made Flesh must surely include the song of the flying birds.

> And from the throne came a voice saying, 'Praise our God, all you his servants, and all who fear him, small and great.' Then I heard what seemed to be the voice of a great multitude, like the sound of many waters and like the sound of mighty thunderpeals, crying out, 'Hallelujah! For the Lord our God the Almighty reigns'. (Revelation 18:5-6)

> The Holy Spirit is the living water 'welling up to eternal life' in the heart that prays. (CCC 2652)

We have always known that Jesus was a Jew. We associate him with Nazareth and Caphernaum in Galilee, and with Bethlehem and Jerusalem in Judaea. As a Jew, Jesus was shaped by the religious faith of his people, and many of his sayings echo those of the Hebrew prophets. Sean Freyne's latest book is called *Jesus, a Jewish Galilean*. Among its many claims is that Jesus' imagination has been shaped very definitely by the Galilean area in which he lived and worked.

Archaeology has uncovered the city of Sepphoris, which lies close to Nazareth. This Roman city was famous for its aqueducts, which brought millions of gallons of water into the fountains and bath houses of the wealthy aristocracy. The effect of this water pilfering must have been enormous on the local peasant farmers, among whom Jesus grew up. Could Jesus be hinting at that water shortage when he offers the Samaritan woman living water that will well up forever?

> Jesus said to her, 'Everyone who drinks of this water will be thirsty again, but those who drink of the water that I will give them will never be thirsty. The water that I will give will become in them a spring of water gushing up to eternal life'. (John 4:13-14)

> Love is the source of prayer; whoever draws from it reaches the summit of prayer. (CCC 2658)

St John Vianney was the Curé in a small French village called Ars, just north of Lyon. Though never famous for his academic ability, he was revered for his wisdom and holiness, and after his canonisation become patron of parish priests. What was the secret of his life? Perhaps the answer lies in his bedroom. There on the wall, side by side, are two simple pictures: one of the immaculate heart of Mary, the other of the Sacred Heart of Jesus.

This prayer comes from the Curé of Ars: 'I love you, O my God, and my only desire is to love you until the last breath of my life. I love you, O my infinitely lovable God, and I would rather die loving you, than live without loving you. I love you, Lord, and the only grace I ask is to love you eternally ... My God, if my tongue cannot say in every moment that I love you, I want my heart to repeat it to you as often as I draw breath' (St John Vianney, Prayer).

> [A]nd hope does not disappoint us, because God's love has been poured into our hearts through the Holy Spirit that has been given to us. (Romans 5:5)

> The prayer of the Church venerates and honours the Heart of Jesus just as it invokes his most holy name. It adores the incarnate Word and his Heart which, out of love for men, he allowed to be pierced for our sins. (CCC 2669)

Like many Irish Catholic families, we had a Sacred Heart picture on our kitchen wall. The figure of Jesus Christ was recognisably foreign and solemn: with bearded features and blazing heart. Underneath were the names of all the children in the house, along with the signature of the local priest. It was not great art, but it was great faith; here we trust in 'the man above', the one who gazes gently down upon us.

We took it all for granted, like bread and butter on the table and parents to provide for all our needs. But the simple icon offered a startling insight: God's care and compassion, so clearly obvious to the Jewish people, went further than anybody expected and took flesh in the person of Jesus. Since the pulse of this God is love, it makes absolute sense to portray the heart of Jesus as a burning offering.

> But when they came to Jesus and saw that he was already dead, they did not break his legs. Instead, one of the soldiers pierced his side with a spear, and at once blood and water came out. (He who saw this has testified so that you also may believe. His testimony is true, and he knows that he tells the truth). (John 19:33-35)

The Holy Spirit, whose anointing permeates our whole being, is the interior Master of Christian prayer. He is the artisan of the living tradition of prayer. (CCC 2672)

The music group from The Mater Dei Institute of Education took part in a celebration of 'creative prayer' in Belvedere College nearby. The accepted wisdom about young people is that they are very open to spiritual matters, provided these echo their life experience. Music plays a major part in youth culture, so it is not surprising that sung prayer makes more sense to young people than standard spoken prayers, to be recited by rote.

'Creative prayer' suggests that this activity is an art form. It suggests the outpouring of a spirit that is creative like the Spirit of God. Too often prayer is seen as a burden, as something we have to do almost against our wills; it is certainly not something to be excited about. Why cannot prayer be recognised for what it truly is: the groaning of God's Holy Spirit, who teaches us what we need to say?

Therefore I want you to understand that no one speaking by the Spirit of God ever says 'Let Jesus be cursed!' and no one can say 'Jesus is Lord' except by the Holy Spirit. (1 Corinthians 12:3)

> Prayer is primarily addressed to the Father; it can also be directed towards Jesus, particularly by the invocation of his holy name: 'Lord Jesus Christ, Son of God, have mercy on us sinners'. (CCC 2680)

It seems that our thought processes cannot function without some reference to the idea of people 'getting what they deserve'. We take a kind of perverse delight in seeing others get what was coming to them. Take the case of the woman caught in adultery. In law, she deserved to be ostracised and, if caught in the act, she deserved to be stoned to death. So why did Jesus not give her what she obviously deserved?

The reason is simple: God doesn't give people what they deserve. God has a quality we call mercy. What interests God is not what people deserve but only what they need. What they deserve is often nothing, but with God this is irrelevant. Only people's needs matter to God, and people always need life, help, support, encouragement and forgiveness. This amazing quality of God, which refuses to think about what people deserve, is called *'trócaire'* in Irish.

> And he said to them, 'I am deeply grieved, even to death; remain here, and keep awake.' And going a little farther, he threw himself on the ground and prayed that, if it were possible, the hour might pass from him. He said, 'Abba, Father, for you all things are possible; remove this cup from me; yet, not what I want, but what you want'. (Mark 14:34-36)

> The church, the house of God, is the proper place for the liturgical prayer of the parish community. (CCC 2691)

Near the centre of Los Angeles there are two churches that differ dramatically. One is on a small street and reflects the Mexican culture of the original missionaries where Spanish is the preferred language. There is evidence of poverty in the streets nearby, but evidence also of compassion for illegal immigrants trying to find a new life in the USA. Hundreds of baptisms take place each Sunday in the plaza beside the main building – a plastic drape offers cover from rain or sun.

Totally different is the new Cathedral, just up the hill. Golden in colour and shaped like a small skyscraper, it evokes the modern American mega-city landscape. Baptisms here take place through immersion in a small pool at the back of the church. A beautiful image of Christ being baptised hangs on the wall above. As the newly baptised walk down the large aisle to the sanctuary area, over a hundred international saints accompany them, all facing forward, towards the altar.

> My soul thirsts for God, for the living God. When shall I come and behold the face of God? My tears have been my food day and night, while people say to me continually, 'Where is your God?' These things I remember, as I pour out my soul: how I went with the throng, and led them in procession to the house of God, with glad shouts and songs of thanksgiving, a multitude keeping festival. (Psalms 42:2-4)

> Prayer is the life of the new heart. It ought to animate us at every moment ... 'We must remember God more often than we draw breath'. (CCC 2697)

Out of the old monastic tradition comes a new work by an English Benedictine, Mark Barrett, entitled *Crossing: Reclaiming the Landscape of Our Lives*. This is an imaginative account of the five common, daily prayer moments that shape the life of the monk. Rising before dawn to pray Vigil the monk is reluctant, unwilling and lacking in any enthusiasm. Later on, at Lauds, there is a more positive feeling that comes with the dawn.

Midday prayer is time out from important work, and a clear reminder that no work is more important than prayer. Evening prayer takes stock of the day, its successes and failures. Compline, before bed, is like letting go of life and moving into death. Though the prayer of monks is unique to their way of life, there are enough points of contact with everyday life for anybody to be able to pray in this spirit. Muslims, too, have learnt this lesson.

> Hide your face from my sins, and blot out all my iniquities. Create in me a clean heart, O God, and put a new and right spirit within me. Do not cast me away from your presence, and do not take your holy spirit from me. Restore to me the joy of your salvation, and sustain in me a willing spirit. (Psalms 51:9-12)

Meditation engages thought, imagination, emotion and desire. This mobilisation of faculties is necessary in order to deepen our convictions of faith, prompt the conversion of our heart and strengthen our will to follow Christ. (CCC 2708)

The Augustinians have a beautiful centre at Orlagh in the Dublin Mountains. On a sunny spring day we met there for an afternoon of relaxation and reflection. Every earlier meeting of the Deanery Support Group was for business, but this was for recreation and meditation, for connecting with our deepest selves and with one another. During the session we could see the sun shining on the centre of Dublin, which we had left behind us for a while.

When the lights began to come on in the city, we knew we were ready to return. As they flickered from the lampposts they said: 'Come back; this is your home; this is where you live and work; this is where God is alive in the struggles of people; this is where darkness often reigns supreme, but where you can be a light to the world'. On the way home, we gathered for a meal.

Again Jesus spoke to them, saying, 'I am the light of the world. Whoever follows me will never walk in darkness but will have the light of life'. (John 8:12)

> Contemplative prayer in my opinion is nothing else
> than a close sharing between friends; it means taking
> time frequently to be alone with him who we know
> loves us (Quote from St Teresa of Avila). (CCC 2709)

The Gospel story of Martha and Mary gives us a
privileged insight into the humanity of Jesus. Tired from
his journeys throughout the Holy Land, frustrated at the
lack of acceptance by many people of his teachings and
badly in need of rest, Jesus often visited his friends
Lazarus, Martha and Mary, who lived near Jerusalem.
Jesus appreciated the welcome he received there and the
food they offered him. But, above all else, he treasured
the listening ear that Mary offered. Her attentive ear was
more helpful to him even than the fine food and wine
that Martha prepared with such diligence.

Martha and Mary can also stand for the two sides to
each person: Martha is the active, busy self, energetic,
productive, efficient, creative and competent. Without
Martha, life would be chaotic. Mary is the reflective,
contemplative, prayerful self. Without Mary life might
be organised, but it could easily lose its soul. Jesus knew
well the importance of both human dimensions. He
regularly worked hard, teaching, arguing, cajoling and
healing people. But he regularly needed time to be
attentive to God the Father in prayer, to listen to the still
small voice of the Spirit welling up within him. Without
his Mary side, could Jesus have been Martha for long?

> Tell me, you whom my soul loves, where you pasture
> your flock, where you make it lie down at noon; for
> why should I be like one who is veiled beside the flocks
> of your companions? (Solomon 1:7)

> Do not be troubled if you do not immediately receive from God what you ask him; for he desires to do something even greater for you, while you cling to him in prayer (Evagrius Ponticus). (CCC 2736)

Before my mother became unable to make big decisions in her own right, owing to her mental incapacity, she gave to me what is called 'enduring power of attorney'. Effectively, this means she trusts me to make these decisions on her behalf, so she has given me the authority to act for her in relation to her property and affairs. The law accepts this transfer of power, because it assumes I will do for her only what is in her best interests.

When Jesus advises us to pray continually and never lose heart, he is inviting us to act in a similarly trusting manner; God, he reminds us, knows what we need, even before we have thought about it. If an unjust judge can be trusted to act in our favour, how much more can we trust the living God to do what is for our benefit. Surely God is more reliable than any human. When we pray each day, we can imagine God as the one who possesses 'enduring power of attorney' in our regard.

> But whenever you pray, go into your room and shut the door and pray to your Father who is in secret; and your Father who sees in secret will reward you. When you are praying, do not heap up empty phrases as the Gentiles do; for they think that they will be heard because of their many words. Do not be like them, for your Father knows what you need before you ask him. (Matthew 6:6-8)

> For 'we have not been commanded to work, to keep watch and to fast constantly, but it has been laid down that we are to pray without ceasing' (Evagrius Ponticus). This tireless fervour can come only from love. (CCC 2742)

In the centre of Milan stands a beautiful Cathedral. It was there, in 387, that the great St Augustine was baptised by St Ambrose, the Bishop of Milan. When I first visited this place, my thoughts moved quickly from Ambrose and Augustine to another person: Augustine's long-suffering mother, Monica. For years she prayed day and night that her son would be converted to the faith, but nothing seemed to happen.

She asked. She sought. She knocked. Eventually, the door was opened. On the feast of Easter, her son walked through the door of the baptistery and was baptised. By persevering in her prayers, even when nothing seemed to be happening, Monica was just like Abraham – his prayer to God on behalf of the sinful people sounds like a haggling session in the market. Eventually after a lot of bargaining, God agrees to do what Abraham asked. Perseverance pays off.

> Pray in the Spirit at all times in every prayer and supplication. To that end keep alert and always persevere in supplication for all the saints. (Ephesians 6:18)

The Lord's Prayer: 'Our Father'

> We can invoke God as 'Father' because he is
> revealed to us by his Son become man and because
> his Spirit makes him known to us. (CCC 2780)

The seminar on the *Catechism of the Catholic Church*
was examining Part Four, which deals with Christian
prayer. This is the shortest but perhaps the most
practical of the four sections. We noted how Luke's
version of the Lord's Prayer is shorter, and so probably
closer to the original than the better-known version in
the Gospel of Matthew. We were struck by the manner in
which the Blessed Trinity is implicit in this great
traditional prayer.

We pray to the Father, using the words given by Jesus his
Son, and our prayer is made through him, with him and
in him. Then we wonder what power it is that binds us
together as we pray in this manner? The answer of
course is the Holy Spirit, who has been poured out upon
us in Baptism and who binds us together into a faithful
community, rooted in God and sharing in God's
inner life.

> In the beginning was the Word, and the Word was
> with God, and the Word was God ... And the
> Word became flesh and lived among us, and we
> have seen his glory, the glory as of a father's only
> son, full of grace and truth. (John 1:1, 14)

> What would he not give to his children who ask, since he has already granted them the gift of being his children (St Augustine). (CCC 2785)

Jesus teaches us how to pray; we should enter into prayer in a spirit of persistence. This is not because God is deaf and has to be told over and over again what we need. Perseverance in prayer is important for our sakes. It is good for us to repeat our requests over and over again so that we can truly discover our real needs, and truly recognise the moment that God grants our petitions.

We should also enter into prayer with a deep sense of confidence in God. Human fathers are generally respectful of children's needs and usually very generous. But God is the 'How much more Father' of the human race. He has already given us a world, a life, a family and friends, a history and a future. The only aspect of this that is still invisible to us is the future. We can afford to hope that the future will not only match the past, but will even surpass our dreams.

> He called a child, whom he put among them, and said, 'Truly I tell you, unless you change and become like children, you will never enter the kingdom of heaven. Whoever becomes humble like this child is the greatest in the kingdom of heaven'. (Matthew 18:2-4)

Our Father calls us to holiness in the whole of our life, and since 'he is the source of [our] life in Christ Jesus, who became for us wisdom from God, and ... sanctification', both his glory and our life depend on the hallowing of his name in us and by us. (CCC 2813)

The Consultation on Adult Faith Formation considered the theme, 'Witnessing to Christ in a world of Religious Pluralism'. It began with a presentation of our favourite images of Christ. There were Russian icons and medieval crucifixes, as well as family photographs and a poem about poor people under a bridge. One of the Indian images was of Christ seated in the manner of Buddha – this was called Christ the Guru. The cultural resonance was outstanding.

In a later reflection on this image, the point was well made that this way of presenting the face of Christ is thoroughly Indian and therefore aptly inculturated. However, this did not prevent the intuition from being appreciated by other cultures. In fact, it was noted that the image of Christ as a teacher of wisdom has very old roots in the New Testament, which describes Jesus as Rabbi or Teacher. This is the title, indeed, with which he is addressed more often than any other.

He said to them, 'When you pray, say: Father, hallowed be your name'. (Luke 11:2)

> In the Lord's Prayer, 'thy kingdom come' refers primarily to the final coming of the reign of God through Christ's return. But, far from distracting the Church from her mission in this present world, this desire commits her to it all the more strongly. (CCC 2818)

Most people expected Kerry to win the 2002 All-Ireland Senior Football final with ease. The footballers from 'the Kingdom' lived up to all expectations in the first half of the game, during which they were obviously the more skilful side. However, a major change occurred in the second half. The Armagh underdogs, undeterred by missing a penalty and failing to score another goal, persisted until they scored the telling goal. From that moment on, they were transformed, and eventually won by a single point.

The support of the saffron clad supporters, who flooded the pitch at full time, was a major factor in this unlikely success. So too was the motivational ability of Joe Kernan, the manager. But perhaps the central fact in this great victory was the sheer determination of the players. They played out of their skins. St Paul would have been proud of them, and might well have encouraged all Christians to learn from the saffron and be as wholehearted in the struggle for God's Kingdom.

> For the kingdom of God is not food and drink but righteousness and peace and joy in the Holy Spirit. (Romans 14:17)

> God wills the salvation of everyone through the knowledge of the truth. (CCC 851)

Jesus talked a lot about God, but he used far more than the normal religious words. He spoke instead about women losing coins in the kitchen and going down on their hands and knees to search for them. He often spoke about shepherds going out to look for a single lost sheep, or about hens gathering their chicks under their wings. He could mention burglars coming to rob a house or kings gathering troops to fight a battle. This was how he regularly talked to people about his Father, God.

I often wonder what he would make of the internet? Would the net remind him of God's universal saving will? Would it suggest to him something of the mysterious Spirit of God who blows where he wills, even though nobody can see him at work? Would it speak to him about the kind of Church he was leaving behind, wherein all are equal as children of God and all can contribute to the health of the body?

> This is right and is acceptable in the sight of God our Saviour, who desires everyone to be saved and to come to the knowledge of the truth. (1 Timothy 2:3-4)

> [Christ] himself is the bread who, sown in the Virgin, raised up in the flesh, kneaded in the Passion, baked in the oven of the tomb, reserved in churches, brought to altars, furnishes the faithful each day with food from heaven (St Peter Chrysologus). (CCC 2837)

Jesus is surrounded by a crowd of hungry people. The location is remote; there are no markets to buy food. Can Jesus do anything for them? First of all, he gets them all to sit down and relax. Then he gets whatever food is available. This he takes in his hands, gives thanks to the Father for all his goodness and, finally, asks his followers to distribute the food to all around him. Nobody is left out. All are included. There are no outsiders in the Jesus meals.

After everybody's hunger is satisfied, there is still an amazing amount of food available. Any thoughtful persons present that day would have noticed how Jesus had behaved just like God the Father. The Jews knew God to be a generous provider. God's blessings had always been much greater than his people expected; God's goodness had been poured out upon them like a flood, no efforts made to be sparing, just a prodigal flow of goodness and blessing.

> I am the bread of life ... I am the living bread that came down from heaven. Whoever eats of this bread will live forever; and the bread that I will give for the life of the world is my flesh. (John 6:48, 51)

> 'And forgive us our trespasses': With bold confidence, we began praying to our Father ... Now, in this new petition, we return to him like the prodigal son and, like the tax collector, recognise that we are sinners before him. (CCC 2839)

When the young man said, 'Give me my share of the property', he was doing the unthinkable. Since property could be inherited only when the father died, the young son was effectively saying to his father, 'I can't wait till you're dead'. He insulted his father in a totally unexpected way. Later, he squandered his money on a life of debauchery. Then he took a job looking after pigs. For Jews, pigs are unclean, and to have any close contact with pigs is wrong.

What about the other son? As the eldest son, he was bound to protect his father's honour. Once the younger son insulted the father, it was expected that the older son would try to make peace between them. But he stood by while his father's honour was destroyed and did nothing – he sinned by serious omission. Later, he did the same at the feast: the older son was supposed to organise all his father's functions, but he was sulking out in the field. What a father! Two ungrateful sons, yet he loves them both and wants them to prosper. If a human father can be like that, what is God the Father like?

> For if you forgive others their trespasses, your heavenly Father will also forgive you; but if you do not forgive others, neither will your Father forgive your trespasses. (Matthew 6:14-15)

> [D]iscernment unmasks the lie of temptation, whose object appears to be good, a 'delight to the eyes' and desirable, when in reality its fruit is death. (CCC 2847)

The Gardaí have been very diligent recently checking the roads for speeding motorists, and there appears to be a reduction in the number of fatal accidents. We should welcome this change. As we congratulate ourselves for this improvement, putting it down to better equipment and more Gardaí on the beat, and as we consider a possible tightening of the law, it is surely time to consider one aspect of the problem that may be overlooked: the individual driver.

For people to drive more carefully, perhaps there is a need for tougher laws. There is definitely a need for better application of those statutes, and perhaps also a need for more investment to improve the standard of our roads. More emphasis on training people to drive properly should also be encouraged. However, fundamentally, how fast people drive is a decision taken by individual drivers each day. Am I prepared to say 'no' to the temptation to speed? Do people even think today about temptation? Do people ever judge themselves to be sinners if they drive too fast?

> But those who want to be rich fall into temptation and are trapped by many senseless and harmful desires that plunge people into ruin and destruction. (1 Timothy 6:9)

> In this final petition [of the Our Father, 'deliver us from evil'], the Church brings before the Father all the distress of the world. (CCC 2854)

A bus mounts the pavement on a Saturday afternoon outside the Clarence Hotel and five people are killed. Unsuspecting travellers are crushed under wheels; many are very seriously injured, and hospital authorities announce one death and fear that others may also die. Families of the dead and injured are in shock and prayers are said at Sunday Masses. The supplier of public transport in Dublin calls for an investigation – this accident is the worst in living memory.

We tend to take a lot for granted; we all assume that bus drivers will be alert, that the busses will run on time and take us efficiently from one part of town to the other. But, even more significantly, we all assume the sun will rise each morning, that our hearts will keep pumping and that the river of life will continue to flow into the sea. We are right to make these assumptions, for we believe in a creator God whose providence guides our daily path. Why do accidents happen to innocent people? Will we ever find out?

> But now I am coming to you, and I speak these things in the world so that they may have my joy made complete in themselves. I have given them your word, and the world has hated them because they do not belong to the world, just as I do not belong to the world. I am not asking you to take them out of the world, but I ask you to protect them from the evil one. (John 17:13-15)